The Green Jeep

Recollections Of A Boy And His Stepfather In Florida Cracker Country

Frank Wesley Williamson, Sr.

Howard S Jones Jr.

Dedication

To Hunter, Madeleine, Catherine, Copeland, Catherine Brennagh, Caedmon, and my covenant son David Schock and his sons, Stratton and Graham. To Sonny and Betty, Kim, Wes, Karen, Heather, John, John Wesley, Brady, Kristin, John Louis, Biba and Charles, Susan, David, the other grandchildren and great-grandchildren and any other souls who like stories about rare people and mended hearts.

Acknowledgements

Many thanks to Adam Christiansen for his guidance in organizing and editing this book and to Hunter, my wife, for her patient proof-reading.

The portraits of Mr. and Mrs. Williamson are by German artist, Gisbert Palmié (1897-1986).
The cover background scene is a reproduction of *The Oak of Compassion* by Robert Butler (1943-), one of Florida's premier naturalist artists.
All are from the author's private collection.

"By Way of a Half-hearted Apology

To the people I have cited both living and dead:
I have borrowed your words, but they <u>are</u> being read.
And if I have misquoted, or mis-spelt a name:
Accept my regrets, my errors—my shame."
-Eliakim Katz

Preface

WHEN I look back on my life, I can see pivotal moments, specific defining times, moments of decision and crossroads. Many of the paths were unmarked, some had clear warnings. Some paths gave no indication of the good that lay around the bends, twists and turns. In retrospect, the surprise is that even wrong choices could lead to glorious pastures of contentment. What at first looked like a dead-end bramble actually was a rabbit trail toward goodness and mercy.

As we mature and look back from the pinnacle of experience, we can see clearly why things went well for us. We see the implications of circumstances and decisions that led to satisfaction, though at the time we were floundering blindly. Hopefully, we learned from the results, both good and bad.

Beyond these moments adventure or disaster awaits. But I am convinced that the hand of God is ever guiding. One of these defining moments in my pilgrimage occurred under an oak tree in June of 1960 in a green Jeep.

I don't know why at this time I suddenly have a need to write about my stepfather. I still think about him a lot. He influenced me for good. He told my mother once, "If I coulda' got to that boy a little sooner, I coulda' saved him a lot of heartache." He never saw me for what I was or had been, he saw me for what I could be. He accepted me warts and all and began a great reclamation. I've written this account as it came to me, often in dialect, but I hope that it communicates his character and the culture in which we lived. You must remember that it is written through the sometimes grimy spectacles of a child who had been badly handled in the early years of his life. Nevertheless, his grandchildren and their children may not remember him well and therefore might benefit from these lame efforts at recording my recollections of him. It may serve as an anchor for their heritage. All who knew him can recall things that were significant to their own lives. These writings are just some of the stories that came to my mind and I wrote them down.

Don't think that I didn't recognize his humanity. Yes, he had his own flaws, as do we all. As the author of The Big Fish said, "It's hard to separate the man from the myth sometimes…" but here, I try. Nor am I making a god of him, although it wouldn't be difficult, as large, not in stature, but in character, as he was. I am just reflecting on the good.

Right before he died, I asked him to give me the most important thing he thought at the time. He replied, "Think good thoughts…your mind will be healthy as a result of all those good chemicals." I expect he knew this area was my own personal demon. The message was for me. It would be different to others who asked. This was the last talk I had with him. His comment was not an idle thing; scientific facts support his advice.

So here in my office, sitting at his old over-sized desk, I write of the humor, pain, revelation, integrity, honor, perseverance, pride and grief in this loving tribute to my stepfather,

Frank Wesley Williamson, Sr.

August, 2009
Brevard, NC

The Introductions

"Above all we must remember at all times what intellectuals habitually forget:
That people matter more than concepts and must come first."
-Paul Johnson, English Historian

THE air was still cool for June in Northwestern Indiana for the Class of '60 Graduation Picnic, which included swimming in the algae-green water of what was once a commercial rock quarry. The park's swimming area was roped off with float barriers. The coarse beach sand had been hauled in. Several picnic tables were scattered here and there on the adjacent grass-carpeted park. The water was so cold that it made our lips blue.

The high dive platform was pretty intimidating, but I jumped anyway, perhaps an indication of the courage needed for the looming upheaval in my life. At the moment life was good but I was anxious about the future. My folks were divorced and I had lived with my Dad in Terre Haute, Indiana, for the past three years, spending only brief summers with my mother in Miami, Florida. My Dad and I stayed in a ten-dollar a week apartment on Maple Avenue at Five Points, about four blocks from Garfield High School where I had just finished. I had decided to stay with him after living a year in Miami with my mother.

Mother had such a hard time when I lived with her. She worked two shifts as a hostess for a large restaurant named Top of The Columbus but took other part time waitress jobs on some days to make ends meet, taking extra work wherever she could find it. She had even worked in a liquor shop at the DuPont Plaza Hotel to see that we had food. This was abhorrent to her. She was torn between selling liquor, which was against her Baptist principles, and caring for me. I remember her inviting me to come to the Seven Seas Restaurant to eat while she was on duty as the hostess. I frequently ate her employee meal at a table right next to the kitchen door. Her boss tolerated me since it was hard to find a reliable hostess. She did without so that I wouldn't have to.

My Dad had no idea of the financial difficulties that we faced while living in Miami. I do not know how I knew that she would do better without me as a responsibility, but I knew. For this reason, plus the Cuban gangs and the "Country-Boy-in-Miami Syndrome," I elected to live with my Dad in Indiana following my eighth school year at Ada Merritt Public School in Miami.

During the three years I lived in Indiana she wrote faithfully. But in the fall of my senior year a letter arrived with unexpected news. She said she had met a fine man and that they were going to get married. I was neutral about the news. Who cared? I was on course for the Air Force, since it was certain that I would soon get an Uncle-Sam-Wants-You letter. Political upheaval in Vietnam was rumbling like distant thunder on the other side of the world, but had little to do with me, so I thought. There was much speculation as to this tiny country's stability and significance in the cold war era. The military draft was real in those days.

Then in February my mother sent a picture. She was standing with her new husband, Frank, and Tom Connelly, an attorney and justice of the peace, before a huge fireplace. The picture showed that the house was still under construction. The new husband wore a white shirt, snappy tie and light blue suit. My mother looked like a million dollars, wearing a big corsage on her shoulder. I didn't show it to my dad. By her description Frank was special. I couldn't imagine what a Florida cowboy was like, especially from the picture.

Mama enclosed some money, which I really needed, and said that they were coming up for my graduation. She also gave me some things to think about. They wanted me to come to Florida, taking some time off before I went into the Air Force.

Two days before graduation, my mother and this man of hers arrived and stayed at the finest hotel in Terre Haute, appropriately named The Terre Haute House. They asked me to meet them that afternoon. I hitched a ride downtown, took a deep breath and went into the lobby. They were there. She was radiant and smiling. Her hair was done and she looked a little like Marilyn Monroe. Yeah, I know that is a stretch but my portrait of her backs me up.

My first meeting was much different from what I expected from the picture she'd sent in February. There in the hotel, next to her was a man of average height, a little stocky. His wavy hair was combed straight back from a slightly receding hairline. He wore Acme Wellington boots and western gabardine pants, held up by a hand-tooled leather belt with a simple buckle. His left hand stuck partway into the slanted pants pocket with only the thumb showing. He apparently was oblivious to the fact that his pants leg was half trapped inside the top of his left boot. He had on a plain white shirt with the top two buttons open. I thought it a bit odd that he was wearing sunglasses in the hotel lobby, but later found out that he had some permanent damage to his sclera from applying sulfur powder and fertilizers to orange groves.

By no means was he sloppy but his unconventional Western wear sometimes caused a double-take in some observers. It was all low-key and tasteful. He was obviously comfortable in his skin, not to mention his clothes. His complexion was a little rough and the lines of his face were deep. He did look like a man who spent a lot of time in the sun. The top half of his face and head were pale from the Stetson he always wore. Above the margins of his shirtsleeves his skin was white. I found out in a day or two that he didn't wear his hat in the hotel but left it resting in the rear window of the car. I was glad to see my mother, but I just didn't know about this man. He shook my bony hand with his thick, rough, calloused one and his first words to me were, "How ya doin', Buddy?" His grip was firm and my hand disappeared in his. Other than that one comment in greeting, he let her do all the talking.

We ate there at the hotel restaurant, a place that I would never have entered in other circumstances. I was experienced in eating in high-end Miami hotels but this was a first there in Terre Haute. They encouraged me to get what I wanted. I tested the waters of this directive, ordering a healthy and expensive steak. It was fine. During the meal he hardly talked at all. He gently agreed with my mother that I ought to take off a few weeks or so, go down to the ranch and take a vacation before going into the Air Force. I agreed. I wasn't really excited about the prospect, but I didn't have anything else pressing me.

What was I getting into? My experience with fathers had not been particularly good. Why should I trust this one? I suppose that I learned early on that I really wasn't worth much. I recall the first time that this message was driven home to me. One early summer day when I was nearly six years old, I asked my mother if I could ride my tricycle around the block. In those days it wasn't unusual for children to do that. She agreed but cautioned me not to cross the street. The roots of giant maple trees raised the sections of the sidewalks, causing my trike to bump heavily, hurting my head. A dull ache was building in my little body. The sunlight was too bright for me that day. The air was cold but my eyes felt hot and sunken. Cutting the trip short, I asked my mother if I could go to bed. She felt my forehead, brought me some juice and tucked me in. I don't remember what happened during the day, but I do remember Dr. Julian B. Cole arrived around midnight. Those were days when family practitioners made house calls. He examined me there in the bed. I felt his cool hands slip under my head as he attempted to push my chin toward my chest. It would not give! My neck and back were as rigid as the proverbial board. He looked alarmed to my little eyes. By this time they felt like they were sunken deep into my head. He asked to use the telephone and quietly told the Methodist Hospital Emergency Room staff to prepare for my arrival. He talked softly to my mother, saying, "I think he has spinal meningitis." Mother started crying, went to the bed where my dad lay sleeping, telling him that she was taking me to the hospital. All I heard was his grumbling, but he didn't offer any help or encouragement. Whether he intended it or it was a totally reflex response, I got the message of rejection that subtly echoed in the hallways of my mind for many years. Even though the significance of this incident lay mostly buried in my little mind, it was decades before I healed, knowingly allowing the pain of this occurrence and many others to slip overboard into the sea of forgetfulness. I don't think he came to any of the series of excruciating spinal taps. I can still envision the pain and the taste of the brand new, life-saving sulfa drug, sulfathiazine. Was this new stepfather more of the same? I surely couldn't tell much at first.

The next day when they picked me up at our shabby apartment, I was surprised by a late model white Cadillac DeVille. I had said my goodbyes to all my close friends and to my dad before he'd gone to work. I think it would have been too uncomfortable for him to see my mother with her new husband. I wondered how he felt when he came home that day to an empty apartment after our three years together. I never asked.

The drive from Indiana to the ranch was awkward. I didn't know what to call him. He was awfully quiet. He exhibited a self-assurance that I was not familiar with. I was a little intimidated by this because I first interpreted it as anger or sullenness. He listened calmly, translating and interpreting me. He already knew things about me I didn't know he knew. He also understood my background, and allowed for it. The first lesson in my journey with him was: he would cut you some slack. I found out later that he had only one hard rule. It actually wasn't hard but it was non-negotiable. I was being studied for my character traits.

We spent the first night in North Carolina in a hotel in Hendersonville, which is not far from where I now live. I never pass that hotel-turned-condominium without remembering that first morning in North Carolina. The air was crisp cold and smelled too clean. It felt like March to me. We had come through Maggie Valley the previous day. That was before Dollywood, about the time that Dolly herself started a career with Porter Waggoner. I don't recall seeing one billboard there, although I see in my mind's eye some roadside Burma Shave and See Rock City signs. It was rustic then—open and charming. I felt like I had come to the end of civilization. The roads were narrow and the traffic was light. We took pictures, touring a bit as we went along. I saw things I'd never imagined before, which wasn't saying much. My world was geometrically expanding.

I'd seen the woods, green pastures and neat farmlands of Kentucky and Indiana. I'd looked at the rolling hills of West Tennessee and North Georgia on the trips to Miami, but here were green mountains with a blue haze over them. The trees grew up right next to the twisting, turning, and gravel back roads with overhanging tree limbs forming dark green tunnels. Here and there would be little cleared farms with rough barns and cabins. The wild flowers, grass and weeds were well established by this time of the year. The farm families built in the lower, protected areas, away from the blasting winter winds, I guessed. Kitchen gardens were just steps away from the houses or cabins and it looked to me as if there was a vegetable-canning area on some of the back porches. A cow, mule, horse or some critter might be ambling around. Old rusty garden farming equipment sat idly near barns or in little attached sheds. Puppies played under dilapidated vehicles or farm equipment. Chickens were doing what chickens do with biddies darting around them like little fish in a pond. It was common to see ladies in colorful bonnets and men in floppy straw hats and bib overalls working in the gardens. There were shallow, rocky-bottomed streams with evidences of high water marks on the trunks of overshadowing trees. All the sights, sounds and smells were surprisingly a soothing balm to my sour soul.

At overlooks, Frank would pull over at the wide spots in the narrow roads. We'd just sit and gaze at the country, enjoying the cool air. For some reason it was natural for me to silently study the mountains, not really interested in saying much. After all, four generations ago my ancestors had passed through these mountains on the way to Western Kentucky.

A cautious healing had begun. Was I being naive? He'd occasionally say things, as if he was concluding inner thoughts, things like, "Boy, a fella would sure have to work hard to make a livin' in these mountains." and "I believe a cow would starve to death here, wooden she?" or "I bet you'd freeze your teehind off here in the winter..." I didn't know what a "teehind" was, but from the context and the country we were looking at, I figured it was related to the posteriors of well diggers in Kentucky. It caused me to smile a little. Well, he did have a sense of humor hidden somewhere behind the dark glasses.

The farther we traveled, the more he loosened up, apparently preferring the more rugged and isolated country. Everything was new to me. How was I to relate to him? I sensed his delight in my wide-eyed enjoyment of these new experiences. We took a back road out of Hendersonville to Saluda, Tryon, Waynesville, Asheville and places I've forgotten. We took our time, but after several days, headed out to Florida.

Needless to say, I was filled with mixed emotions. Things were changing a little too fast. What had I gotten into? Still I had the distinct feeling while riding in the back seat, there was more than meets the eye in this man. My mother seemed very content. What was going on behind his sunglasses and panatela cigars? Why was he so quiet and deep in thought at times? Were the few funny things he said just for my benefit? Was he just reserved or really sullen and angry? I wished I was a better judge of character.

Heading for Okeechobee

"They call it Okeechobee City now but once hit wer' known as Tantie, the wildest settlement east of the Mississippi. Hit was surrounded by cow camps on the north, by sawmills on the east and by cat fish camps on the lake and between the cow hunters, the wood choppers and the catfish boys, when things got to goin' good in Tantie, mister, if you think that wadn't a rip roaring, hell raising town, hits jus' because you ain't never been ther."
-Lawrence E. Will, in, *A Cracker History of Okeechobee*

OUR destination was the Caloosa Ranch, about seven miles north of a little Florida town called Okeechobee City. Okeechobee has had a colorful history. It was established several miles north of Lake Okeechobee in 1915. The lake, which is the second largest within a state, is some seven hundred square miles in size and so wide you could see a slight curve on its horizon. The shallow lake, twelve to fourteen feet at its deepest, is notorious for its boat-swamping waves when the winds gather them and send them rolling. The black waters of Taylor Creek run a meandering southern course on the eastern side of the town on the way to the lake. The settlement was first founded by catfishermen, cattlemen and homesteaders. It has been said that escaped slaves and criminals from chain gangs came down from Georgia in the early days. Nobody ever asked where you came from then. Nobody wanted anybody to know. In those days people could just disappear in the wildernesses of Florida, found only if they allowed it.

Arcadia, first called Tater Hill Bluff, was located some thirty-five miles to the west and, in contrast to Okeechobee, was a pure cattle town. It had outlaw gangs who were cleaned out by locals in a famous gunfight that gets reenacted every year at the Arcadia Rodeo. Tater Hill was the home of Bone Mizell who died of "moonshine—went to sleep and did not wake up." If you kept driving straight through Arcadia, you'd end up in Bradenton, at the time, a small quiet Gulf coast town due south of Tampa. To the east lay Ft. Pierce, a place where the old Cracker families sold cattle for shipping to Cuba and other places.

Okeechobee was a rough and ready town in the early part of the 20th century, all the way up until the sixties, but even in my day, you could still get your "head skint" on a Saturday night at places like the Twin Oaks Cafe. Someone once said a man ran into the kitchen there, asking where the back door was. The cook said they didn't have a back door, to which the man replied, "Wher' do ya want one?" Locals said there was a knifin' or a killin' almost every weekend in the forties.

A railroad came down from New Smyrna, going almost directly north and south throughout most of its course to the early settlement of Okeechobee. It actually turned a little to the southwest near a long abandoned turpentine settlement named Opal, which was on the ranch we were headed for. The railroad delivered supplies, then returned with iced-down barrels of catfish. Those were the days when the engine's top speed was about 30 miles per hour on a good day. Crackers would jump on somewhere, ride to a suitable hunting area and jump off. They'd flag the returning train, pay a fee of one or two turkeys or a haunch of venison and return home.

There was a natural enmity between the catfishing and the cowboy crowd. It was similar to that involving dogs and cats. People usually minded their own business. There were social gatherings, "jooking," pool-playing and times in town where idle people sat under the oaks at the wide main street mall, reading the newspaper or a dime novel, chewing tobacco or smoking, or just whittling and talking. It was not unusual in those early days to see small Cracker horses tied to the bumpers of Model-T's or to low-hanging oak limbs. Palmettos grew right up next to the jooks and stores, the jail and even near the courthouse. Palmettos grew everywhere in town. While a visitor would notice them everywhere, the locals just didn't pay any attention to them. Where they were not rooted up with grubbing hoes and burned they minded their own business next to the older established buildings, harboring mice, quail, spiders, gopher tortoises, blue-tailed lizards and chameleons. Even a rattlesnake or two used them for shelter. As things began to modernize in the forties and fifties, land was cleared for new establishments. Palmettos and the critters they protected gave way to shops, stores, drug stores, cafes, a bank, groceries, hardware and western wear stores, and a church or two.

In the sixties, Okeechobee was at first glance a clean, sleepy little town. Most shops and stores closed on Wednesday afternoons for folks to take care of "other business", i.e., fishing, hunting, gardening, napping, sitting around on park benches or porches and whittling or repairing a truck or saddle. According to the ol' timers, it wasn't unusual to come to town and see men, one boot cocked on the running board of an old truck or jalopy, straw cowboy hats tilted up on their heads, just talking and enjoying the moment. Life was too short and the summers too hot not to take time to visit now and then. It was a time of conversation and storytelling. Most of the citizens of Okeechobee worked hard but generally enjoyed each other's company when they could. However, things were beginning to change in the sixties.

Farther south in Florida, especially on the east coast, land became too precious for dairy or beef cattle ranching. Offers too good to refuse were accepted. Dairies and ranches began to purchase large tracts in Okeechobee County. Places where Florida scrub cattle had roamed for many years now had fenced-in pastures holding black and white Holsteins. Large milking barns and bright new-wood cow pens dotted the landscape. Folks smelling like big money moved in, buying up pastureland. Yes, things were beginning to change in Okeechobee.

In ever increasing places old marl roads gave way to hard-topped roads. Marl, the basic foundation of these roads was a mixture of sand, clay, calcium carbonate and seashells. It compacted well but could be sticky after a rain, especially if it had little sand and shell in it. The marl/sand roads appeared suddenly. You'd drive off the hard top with a little bump, and continue on the marl roads. Your tires would make a unique, steady cracking and crunching sound as you drove over them. They were bright roads in the sun, making you squint in the reflected sunlight. They had potholes where rainwater collected. But in the earlier days, all the roads were sand only.

There were no hitching posts, but it was almost like there should have been. It was a town with a truly pioneer flavor, and we were heading straight for it! When Frank and Mother talked about it on the way, it sounded almost like a foreign country. Would this trip be something good or a bust? I had no idea. It would only be a short visit and I could tolerate just about anything for a limited period. I did not know what would happen...I was along for the ride. It might not even be worth unpacking my meager belongings.

That first night in Florida, we drove in on U. S. 441 late, going through a place called "Yee Haw Junction." I remember a honky-tonk on the ground floor of a hotel with a few raggedy trucks and cars out front. For some reason the marquee lights, better known as, "tha porch lites", were all green neon, kind of gaudy and flashy. It looked like a western saloon. Just a few hundred yards south of that intersection, things went back into rough. The grass on the right of way was uncut and as tall as a horse's belly. The lights of the car shined it up. We rode with the windows down and said little during the last hour or so. The frogs and crickets were getting ready for the big summer; for them time was a-wastin'. There was a slight lowering in pitch of their calls as we passed passels of them, like the sound of a train passing a station platform. I smelled new things, like soured grasses and stale water. Water had backed up in places next to the roadway. This was June in Florida when rainwater filled the ditches, creeks, ponds and swamps. They were flashing by in the headlight beams as we moved over the county line into Okeechobee County. When we passed a body of water, even a small one, the frog calls were decidedly louder. I had the feeling that the land was getting slightly lower as we left Yee Haw, but that could have been only an impression. Every now and then there was the faint smell of fresh cow manure or some poor bug hitting the windshield. But mainly I remember the tall grass in the headlights, the frogs calling for mates, and the moist warm night air. You couldn't see very far into the pastures, but you just knew there was something out there.

I observed that he drove awfully slowly, looking ahead into the dark night as if lost in thought. I expect our top speed was about 50 mph. The closer we got to Okeechobee, the more relaxed he became. I would learn that he regularly did this deep-thought business, able to shut out all noise, concentrating on some plan. He never seemed to be in a hurry. I slipped my hand out the window, absentmindedly letting it soar up and down, just absorbing the newness of it all.

The air was warm, humid and thick in this thinly populated area. It stretched out forever ('course, Yee Haw *is* in the middle of nowhere). There was little traffic. I just didn't expect this, as my only experience in Florida was Miami—still a sleeping giant in 1956. We came onto the marl ranch road about midnight. Here, too, the grass was cricket-infested, tall and thick. Just before we got to the turnoff to the ranch there was a pasture on the left. I later remembered it as a place my mother and I had passed on the way to Miami some 3 years earlier. I recognized it because as we were going to Miami in a 1949 Plymouth, there was a herd of cattle pushed up to the fence, being driven to a pasture north of the ranch. It burned into my mind since it was so striking. I can't remember faces but I remember the cowboys "boogerin'" the herd with hats, whips and coiled ropes.

"Boogering" is a Cracker term I learned which means startling cattle into moving along more quickly. Its meaning may or may not be evident, according to one's upbringing. It's used loosely in several ways. "Spook" is a synonym. I've seen restless herds or fidgety animals that would "booger" at the slightest sound. And I've seen old tame cattle like dairy cows who would take prodigious "boogering" to get them going. Apparently a "boogeror" is the one making the noise to "booger" the cattle; a "boogeree" is the one "boogered" and a "boogerette" is a small girl on horseback "boogering" cattle. "Boogery" was used to indicate that something, like a dark approaching thunderhead, was scary or threatening. "Plum boogery" was the term for "terrifying". The cattle were so tightly bunched that they were making the fences squeak as they crowded against the wooden posts and fence wire. Their tails were swishing. Their horned heads were held high and Brahma ears were flipping nervously. There was the smell of cattle, of heated bodies and medicinal dip. It's funny how you remember smells. I marveled at this but never thought that I would later become accustomed to them. I never would have expected to see the ranch again that I had seen some three years earlier on Highway 441, just north of a little town named Okeechobee. Small world, isn't it?

We pulled into the garage of a large dark house. It smelled of new paint and wood. I was shown to a room on the first floor where I unpacked a few things. We ate a late supper, bacon and eggs, I think. I walked around in the large living room. It reminded me of a resort, having an enormous brick fireplace and an 18 to 20-foot high beamed ceiling. It was warm, with comfortable and inviting over-stuffed furniture, wide Cypress board paneling, and cool tile floors throughout. The whole house was an attractive blend of southern and western styles. There was a faint smell of wood smoke from the fireplace. The mantle was a six-inch thick deep orange-red board hewn from heart of pine, also called "lighterd," or "pine fatwood." Over the mantle was the biggest set of steer horns I'd ever seen. Measuring some fifty-two inches from tip to tip, they were shaped like the classical horns of the Mexican fighting bull, but much less forward-pointing and much wider. They fit the fireplace and mantle.

Smokey, Frank and Reeda

My room was modestly furnished and had north- and east-facing windows. I kept hearing calves bawling outside. What in the world was that about? I looked but it was pitch dark. I couldn't see a thing but yard grass and a faint fence outline through trees at the edge of the yard. I could hear rustling in the palm trees and the sharp crack-snap of breaking branches. I didn't understand why there was all this activity in the middle of the night. I remember falling asleep to the soft lows of the calves. I found out in the morning that these were freshly weaned calves and were missing their mamas pretty badly. Their separation from the familiar was very much like what I was experiencing, as well.

The next morning I looked out the window the first thing since the calves were still upset. I shall never forget that sight. There was a huge marsh pasture with cabbage palms clustered next to the fence a short distance from the house. The house was situated in a cabbage palm hammock. Hammocks, originally called "hummocks" by the Spanish, are little ground rises. There are oak and cabbage (palm) hammocks, and pine islands where the soil and flora are different from scrubs, swamps, bays, pastures and marshes. The weanling pasture was a part of the hammock and served as some shelter for them. Out in a little adjacent pasture, about two to three hundred yards away, was the dump where we burned trash. Later, it would be a weekly chore for me to load all the garbage cans into the back of the Jeep and head out there.

After breakfast I went outside. The palms and myrtle bushes had hidden much of the view of the marsh pasture the night before. It was larger than it had appeared at first from the bedroom window. There were green pasture as far as one could see. It was about 700 acres. In the distance you could see a tree line. There were orange-winged crows and meadowlarks out and about. The weanlings were still a bit restless, even after a full night of bawling for mama, but most of them had given up the search, eating grass or resting while chewing the cud. The air was already warm. Up in the cabbage palms, hidden in the boots of the branches, little green tree frogs were calling out to no one in particular. Maybe you had to be a frog to fully appreciate their songs.

I went through the house to the garage, noticing the green Jeep that I hadn't seen in the dim garage light the night before. It was there, but I didn't pay much attention to it. Had I only known what its significance would become to me, I would have shown more reverence and respect. I love Jeeps today because they bring back good memories, though there are those times I remember getting stuck in a bog. I had to walk back to the house many a time at night after trying a bad place. Paw observed, "If there is a bad place on this ranch, that boy can bog a Jeep or a tractor in it." He would drive me back to the bog to pull me out. I had a lot of learning to do when it came to where Jeeps and tractors could and could not go. I don't feel too bad because Sonny, the new stepbrother, was with me sometimes, encouraging me, "I think we ought to try it. We can make it." And he was slightly older, more experienced than I was, but nonetheless, I testify here that he could stick a Jeep up as well as anybody. The trash area back of the house is significant because a funny thing happened there once, in fact, several funny things happened in the green Jeep. I'll tell you about them later.

The Ranch

"Lake Okeechobee's back country for 25 or 30 miles on all its northern side was both prairie land and pine. These prairies of wire grass and sedge, the grazing grounds for cattle, were unbroken except for patches of flat wood where towering pitchy pines, 15 inches in diameter and 75 to 100 feet in height grew on slightly higher ground. In places, crossing these flat woods, were heads of cypress and small trees growing in shallow sloughs. Dotting the prairie were numerous small ponds called according to the growth found in each one, sawgrass ponds, flag ponds, or maiden cane..."
-Lawrence E. Will, in *A Cracker History of Okeechobee*

IN 1941, four and a half months before Pearl Harbor, Frank Williamson came to Okeechobee to manage a new federal agricultural development program. He at first had a job with the Farm Security Administration, but was transferred to this new post. The mandated objective was a cooperative effort to develop activities in all fields of Southern agriculture. According to the Okeechobee News article of July 25, 1941, the program was to provide support and the enabling of first-time small operators entering the cattle business. So the Dixie Cattlemen's Association was organized with $794,250 of Federal capital, all ear-marked for investment in land and equipment. Adjusting for inflation, when daily wages for hard labor might run $2.00 or less, this was a considerable sum. One hundred twenty-five families joined the association.

The Association, under Frank's management, purchased a vast tract of land across the entire county, going east to west. I have heard that the purchase was 100,000 acres, but the newspaper article indicated it was about 75,000. This was a period when most people thought of Florida as mostly an assortment of wealthy tourist wintering places. Everything else was swamp or mosquito-infested wilderness. They weren't far off in that estimation.

Land development was one of the first priorities. Wild tough cattle, probably descendants of those abandoned by early Spanish explorers, still ran loose on portions of the vast property. Their value, if you could have caught them, might have been at most a few dollars a head. Hiring hands, fencing, pasture planting and cattle management began in earnest. Camp houses, cow pens, traps for holding cattle and a headquarters had to be built. One problem became immediately apparent: there was no good way to sell your cattle. The Association, under his direction, built the first auction market in Okeechobee County. It was opened for business on July 9, 1942. On August 14, 1942, the Okeechobee News reported, "Manager Frank Williamson stated that small ranchers are receiving, for the first time, a fair and equitable price. The top price for calves was $10.40 per hundred pounds." Sixty-five years later, the now privately owned Okeechobee Livestock Market is still in operation.

Just after WW II, the mood of the nation and government were changing. This was the era of McCarthyism, when backlash swept through the country. For this and other reasons, Congress ordered the systematic shutdown of all kinds of cooperative programs, including The Dixie Cattlemen's Association of South Florida. The land and assets were offered for sale to the public. Frank recognized the potential of the property; he'd ridden horseback through just about all of it. So after considerable time and effort, he and a friend, Johnny Edwards, bought a large portion of the original tract. They split the assets in 1948, with the Caloosa Ranch being about 10,000 acres on the east side of Highway 441. Johnny Edwards took the portion west of the highway.

Frank maintained an outside vocation as an agricultural appraiser, plowing earnings back into repaying the loan and developing the ranch. Marshes were drained, flood-control plans established, fences and cow pens built, and access roads carved out of the dense hammocks. Riding on horseback ahead of the dozers clearing brush and trees, he scouted for the best route of the roadway, one which allowed for high water times and minimal destruction of the woods and wildlife areas. He discovered a particular oak sapling, just stirrup-high, which had a perfect shape. It was square in the path of the proposed access road. Leaning from his saddle he tied his handkerchief to the top branch, turned back and alerted the dozer driver to reroute the road and leave the little tree alone. Asked why he singled out this one specimen, he replied simply, "It'll be a fine oak someday." And it is; perhaps serving as a living monument to his sense of stewardship, character, wisdom and foresight.

Twenty-odd years later, Robert Butler, who had from childhood regularly painted scenes of the ranch, was commissioned by the family to capture that tree on canvas as a Christmas gift for me and my little family. He gave it the title, "Oak of Compassion," alluding to the talk Paw and I had in my early years on the ranch. I don't know who initiated the idea, but that picture is as priceless and precious to me as any material thing can be.

At some later time he divided the property into two parts: the Caloosa Ranch to the east of the old railroad grade, and the Williamson Ranch to the west, which I think he retained as personal property. Many years later the Caloosa was incorporated into Williamson Ranch, but just recently it has been re-established as a business entity. The brand of the Caloosa was The Bent Arrow, a slightly bent featherless arrow. The Williamson brand was called a "T-O", and looked like a T that has been cut mid-stem with an overlapping O inserted in the middle of the stem. In other words, the top of the shortened T showed above the inserted O and a short bottom of the T shown below the O.

I was unaware of these sorts of details at the time. Bits and pieces of the history would come to light in abbreviated fashions, only here a little and there a little over the next few years. I suppose that he thought it would be construed as bragging if he were to go into detail. Besides, I had no need for explanations at this point. I was just in it for the short haul.

The Green Jeep

The Green Jeep

"To be human is to live with the offer of that sonship or daughterhood as the destiny for which we were created and to which we can by grace be restored."
- Donald T. Williams, *Mere Humanity*

MY first full day on the ranch was a "Ten" on the Awe Meter. I couldn't believe my world had been so turned upside down. Beginning in the rolling hills of Western Kentucky, until age fourteen, to the streets of Miami, to the flatlands of Northwestern Indiana, I now found myself in cattle country in South Florida – all occurring in a short eighteen years. Here, I had been transported to a strange new world. I remember "the step-father" asking me if I wanted to go riding on the ranch with him. I asked where we were going. He replied, "Oh, just out. Take a look around." Well, I didn't know what we would do. As it turned out, we made the look-around in the green Willis Jeep. It was a rather plain stripped-down, no frills model and, though fairly new, already had signs of rough use. Later, the all-inclusive cowboy phrase would sum it up for me, "It reminds me of an ol' gal I once knew" which meant that it had seen better days. And you know the expression, "Rode hard and put up wet?" That fit, too. You'da thought a man who drove a brand-new Cadillac would have had a fine new shiny something for the ranch. This one was dark-green with an off-white fiberglass hard top. There was a back window that could be closed against the tailgate, but it usually was slid up and fastened out of the way under the back roof of the cab. The handle stuck out a little so you could stand on the tailgate and hold it for a ride. The sides of the back cab were a nondescript gray. It had no doors and the wheels were caked with the ubiquitous mixture of marl, shell and sand, which was flung up on the sides of everything that ventured off the blacktopped roads. The back deck wore some deep scratches, as if from a roll of barbed wire. Throughout the Jeep's bare metal floor were chunks of dried mud, muck, sand and the remains of leaves and twigs – the flotsam and jetsam of a hard-worked vehicle. Evidently no one had given a thought to cleaning it inside or out. It looked like what it actually was – just a tool, a means of transportation. Little did I know how prized this object of benign neglect would become to me, serving as the fuel for a lifetime of memories.

To most people it was just an old green Jeep. To me it became a sanctuary, a haven and a good friend. I never thought of taking a picture of it. Now I wish I had. It smelled like dogs. Years later I managed to own one very much like it.

Frank had three of the canine creatures who eyed me suspiciously, especially since I was taking the passenger seat that had apparently belonged to one of them. They had already worked out a pecking order among themselves. The seat's springs were sagging somewhat, and fit Dot the English Pointer's butt perfectly. I am sure that is what caused it to sag in precisely that way. If you sat just right, it fit a human butt as well. As the Jeep aged, this sagging spot became much more pronounced. Shorty was a black and brown Beagle, a little pot-bellied and heavy, but he had a good nose. It was hard for him to jump into the Jeep. Smokey, the Weimaraner was the leader.

There was no back seat, which suited the dogs just fine because it gave them plenty of room to jump in and rest while the trip went on. I'd swear those dogs could easily run over 20 miles a day. Occasionally there were tense moments when something caught their interest. They would jack-knife off the back of the Jeep, righting themselves in the air and landing at a run toward a squirrel, armadillo, fox, turkey, or the like. But they usually trotted alongside or in front of the Jeep at a steady pace. You could stretch out the side of the Jeep and touch them. Dot had a habit of picking up a leaf or stick and carrying it for a while or jumping up into the open rear of the Jeep with it – that's where a good bit of the floor trash came from. The other dogs would return with an occasional trophy from a side trip, a small armadillo or such, and would hold it in their mouths as they ran. This eventually wore the points off their canine teeth. The armadillos were usually released unharmed, but puzzled, when some other treasure took the honored carrying position.

Frank would race the motor with the clutch in to alert the dogs, "Git out the way!" How we kept from killing them was a factor of anticipation on their part and the consistency with which the driver drove. Sometimes, the dogs disappeared for several minutes. I was a little concerned at first, but then here they would come from a palmetto patch on one side or another; often they took short cuts to meet the Jeep farther around the bend. They could predict with knowing accuracy the route of the Jeep. Not long after I started these daily round-abouts, I noticed there was a particularly huge fox squirrel residing on the west side of the ranch, near the land donated to the Florida School for Boys. This beautiful brown squirrel, with a reddish blond tail, had a thing for racing the dogs to a tree. He'd get out just far enough in the open pasture to make the ensuing chase sporting, then dart back at the last minute with Smokey, Dot and Shorty hot at his heels. He would climb at least ten feet up the tree to safety, as Smokey had once pulled a sizable amount of tail hair out when Mr. Squirrel had underestimated his height.

This almost daily taunting was a standard activity until one day, whether planned or happenstance I don't know, the dogs out-foxed the squirrel on the daily run. Smokey ran way down the road, no doubt in pursuit of something he'd spotted ahead, while Dot trotted with the Jeep. Pot-bellied Shorty was dragging up the rear, as usual. It must have come to Smokey's mind that he had by-passed the racing area because he turned back, coming from the south, through the pasture. Dot had already registered for the race, drawing the attention of the squirrel. Shorty was trying to make up lost ground by cutting across the pasture from another direction. Being a beagle, he could not help himself; he opened with excited yaps, barking about every three strides. Mr. Squirrel spotted Dot entering the pasture. Figuring she was the only entry that day, he just sat there, eyeing her with what was probably an amused expression, only slightly distracted when Shorty started barking. It did not occur to him that Smokey, the fast tail biter, was closing in on him from behind. At the last possible second Mr. Squirrel turned to dart to a nearby tree, but instead saw a gray blur bearing down on him. He swerved away and headed an entirely different direction, just in time to meet ol' Shorty, who had cut across. Dot was closing in, too. As if it were happening by script, all three dogs simultaneously descended on Mr. Fox Squirrel, all tumbling in a pile of paws, various colored hairs and exploding specks of sand and saliva. I was fascinated as we stopped to watch the fray. From amid the wad of canines, in the hesitation and confusion and blur of dog's legs, the squirrel made it out, dashing in sharp zigs and zags toward a nearby pine sapling, the best he could do on such short notice. He made it with barely room to spare. All three dogs circled the spindly tree with delighted barking and wildly wagging tails. The squirrel nervously "chip-chipped". Frank chuckled that the dogs had never been this close to him before and didn't know what to do once they got him caught. Up until this time it was a harmless ritual for them, but it was a little too close for the squirrel's comfort that day. The dogs loved it.

Frank never drove the Jeep faster than dogtrot speed. In fact, about every week or so he'd drive it to town to get the mail at the same pace. I never was comfortable with the cattle trucks and eighteen-wheelers blasting up behind us. In reply to my concerned comments, he'd say, "I pay my taxes so I can drive as slow as I want to." On these trips we'd get the Jeep up to 40 or even 42 mph. It would spit and sputter some, blowing black carbon out the tailpipe. Somehow it would maintain this speed and settle down to a modest third-gear hum on the highway.

Every now and then when we'd start off to town, he'd push in the clutch and race the motor. Black billowing clouds would belch out from the insult. (Isn't this called an "Italian Tune-up"?) You always hoped you were upwind during these proceedings. The Jeep would sound asthmatic for a while then it would settle back into its routine operational mode. "Jus' cleaning out the carbon," he'd say. He'd ride with his left foot on the clutch pedal. Eventually, the clutch plates became so worn that if he hit a little dip in the road, it'd slip, and the motor would race spastically before it caught again. He was never aware of this habit. The rubber pad was considerably worn where his foot rested. I believe he liked the Jeep as well as he did his old hat.

I don't remember all the details of those first few days. I know I was overwhelmed. I asked some questions which he answered directly. What kind of oranges are those? Was this an old homestead? What in the world dug that hole? Does that dog bite? You really have wild turkeys run in front of the Jeep? And many other questions. Sometimes he would volunteer information. Most of the time the information was very practical, but his brevity threw me off a little. Was he mad with me for some reason? Sometimes it would be offered with a twinkle in his eye. He told me of a man that asked him what that "red thing was behind the trees". He said, "That's the setting sun." The man came back with another question: "Does it always set there?" Later the same man asked what that little circular area in the pasture was. Frank replied, "It's a pond full of rainwater." To this the man asked, "Does it just rain right there?" He laughed when he told about it – but he didn't ridicule. He just enjoyed it. At least none of my questions were of this caliber. I soon understood his dry humor and "leg-pulling." You had to watch him real close or you would miss the wit. After a few days I grew accustomed to these trips and looked forward to them.

It sounds funny, I guess, but Mama and I were like two kids when we rode with him in those early days – we were rather giddy. We acted more like brother and sister than son and mother. We each took turns sitting on the hood of the Jeep, hooking our heels behind the bumper. I particularly liked to ride there. Frank would putt-putt around, looking past me, watching for dogs that cut across the road. If I wasn't riding there or in the passenger seat, I would stand on the lowered tailgate, holding the little handle of the stowed back window, balancing, swaying and trying to anticipate when a dog would jump past my legs to get in the Jeep for a rest. There was an old .22-caliber rifle in the Jeep, propped on its barrel between the front seats. The barrel eventually wore off where it rested on the floor board, the sand and jostling motion acting like a grinding wheel. That .22 had a little scope on it. Mama liked to shoot it. She missed a lot but enjoyed trying it anyway.

Frank told me to ride up front on the center of the hood. I carried the .22 with me there, looking for armadillos. We did have a problem with them. The holes they dug, sometimes running thirty feet in length, have broken the legs of many fine horses, tumbling the riders, as well. These burrows were safe houses for rattlers and gopher tortoises, serving as protection from fires started by lightning. The dang things supposedly entered Florida from a pair that escaped from a Texas sideshow carnival in Tampa. Armadillo females produce identical quadruplets. This ability to proliferate is the reason they spread so quickly in ideal environments. Armadillos like to get out and about after rains, at twilight and dark, rooting and tearing up the ground for insects. Though especially active after a rain, they predominantly work the evening and night shift. When you were alone in the woods, in the pitch dark of night, your imagination would run wild for they made an inordinate racket while foraging for bugs. We tried to control excessive numbers as they were taking over the place, causing hazards in the pastures. The only things that destroyed St. Augustine pastures worse than armadillos were little herds of wild hogs.

I remember asking my mother if she wanted to swap with me to ride up on the hood. Apparently this impressed him. He later said, "Boy, I never saw anybody quite like you--ridin' up on the hood was right down your alley, but you asked your mama if she wanted to take your place." Frank would occasionally ask me, "Which direction is the house?" I'd point and he would confirm or deny my choice. I guess he knew I would need that skill at some future time.

By the end of the first week, I had met Sonny, my stepbrother, and Betty, his wife. I wouldn't get to meet Biba and Charles for another month. I met Hubert Waldron, Harris "Partner" Sills, Lyle, the tractor driver and mechanic, and two men named Jesse: "Purty-Jesse" and "Ugly-Jesse". Jesse Potts, the younger of the two, stayed on the ranch for many more years. The standing joke was when you'd ask them which one was "Ugly Jesse", they'd point to the other one. James Shaw was there shortly after I arrived. I've forgotten the last name of the other Jesse. The men were polite but mostly business when "Mr. Frank" drove up. Sometimes we'd park a little ways back from the activities, sitting in the Jeep and watching the men putting out fertilizer, hoeing trees, shoveling, pruning citrus trees, unloading supplies, or doing tractor work. Hubert ran the dragline, using it to clean canals for drainage and flood or water control.

At first I didn't have much to say. The men were curious about me, asking all sorts of questions. "Wher' you from?" was the number one question for awhile. Partner was friendly, as was Purty and Ugly Jesse, while Hubert didn't say much. Once introduced to this strange new world of openly friendly people, I began to relax a bit. Though still wary, I felt like my scars didn't show so much. Maybe they just overlooked them. I didn't know. All I knew is that emotionally I was one lost, whipped puppy.

Our Defining Talk in the Green Jeep

MANY of the details of those first few days at the ranch have slightly dimmed. I know I was overwhelmed with the different plants, wildlife and environment. We rode through muck marshes, dark tree- and vine-tangled hammocks, under cabbage palms, oaks, maples, myrtles and bay galls. Some of the daily trips took us through thick places where the tree limbs and bushes would spring into the Jeep, slapping the taste out of your mouth.

There were several types of Florida land on the ranch: pine flatwoods, wetland marshes, some with and without muck bottoms, and swamps, which included bay and myrtle trees, bogs and standing water. Frank explained that the black muck was actually layers of decayed and compacted vegetation, accumulated over decades and centuries. Deep and soft in places, it would stick like tar to the wheels, trapping a car or tractor if it was really wet. Cypress swamps were predominantly cypress trees and knees with cabbage palms intermingled throughout. Oaks, cabbage palms and palmettos here and there made up the hammocks, usually a little higher than the surrounding land, thus making them ideal for plants and trees that didn't tolerate being submerged in water. Most of the trees could take flooding for a short time, especially citrus trees, but long-term flooding would kill them. In other areas the sand was like white table sugar. Here palmettos, little gnarled scrub oaks and knotty yellow pines covered many of the so-called Florida Scrubs. Where the bare sand shone in a glare of white, not much grew. It took time to establish the scrub plants, but here and there little islands of hardy adapted plants took hold. They did well if left alone.

As the land gradually rose, pine and palmettos with a dash of other plants, like myrtle bushes, took charge of the land. Some of these high places at one time had solid masses of pines so high and thick that the sun didn't touch the earth under them. Frank said you could see a buck flag as he ran for a long distance under theses pine canopies, as it stood out on the brown floor of fallen pine needles. Where water frequently flowed and receded, where the pines, palmettos and other plants thrived, at times the water would surround these elevated clumps of pines. These were called "pine islands" for the obvious reason they looked like islands in the high water. Frank mentioned, more than once throughout the years, "It takes a good piece of earth to shove up a big healthy pine tree." Here and there lone dead pines and resin-filled stumps, trunks and knots, called literd, could be seen amid the trees. Further north and west of the ranch there was another land type called the Big Indian Prairie. This was a vast true prairie with ponds, little natural drainage ditches and clumps of low growing palmettos, wild flowers, native grasses and other adapted plants. The soil was thin and sandy. It had been fertile, but one-time farmers had cleared and planted, adding nothing back to the soil, and the productiveness was soon lost, making subsequent crops pitiful at worst and uneconomical at best. Replanting was not worth the effort.

Each type of land harbored a population of creatures all its own. The fearless Florida Scrub Jays lived only in the scrubs with the gopher tortoises, snakes and lizards. Deer, turkeys, raccoons, panthers, bear and a host of birds and little creatures roamed the rest.

Frank told me about "muck fires" started from lightning or from intentional fires used for pasture management. He indicated that when burning pastures, people had to be sure that the grass would burn and the muck was damp. I was amazed to hear of muck fires burning for months, leaving large, burned out holes beneath a thin layer of charred grass and muck, an imminent danger to unsuspecting drivers. Sometimes tons of water or even rain would not extinguish the fires. They just had to burn themselves out. South Florida residents smelled the smoldering muck fires as far as fifty miles away or more.

I was amazed to see old, very old, sour orange and wild grapefruit trees, some fifty to seventy-five years in age, as a matter of fact. They were feeble but still had fruit hanging on scrawny limbs. Once in a while, he'd stop the Jeep in the deep hammocks, pull the .22 out and shoot a couple of grapefruit out of the branches. They would thump on the ground with a shattered stem and a few leaves still in place. He'd cut out a plug with his pocketknife, hand it to me and prepare another. We'd suck the juice. They were a little tart but tasty. We rode through knee-deep black water, following submerged trails, the water sometimes reaching the floor of the Jeep. Every now and then we'd hit a submerged hole or rut, upsetting the dogs and the contents of the Jeep, including the passengers. The steering wheel would jerk wildly as the Jeep crawled over bushes, logs and small trees.

There was something wondrous about riding over various natural cow trails in the water. The Brahma cattle were noted for their single-file paths. The wheels made a swishing sound on the wet grass, like tires on sleet. In deeper water the wake would radiate out from the Jeep, making grass and water plants tremble, and move on into dark underbrush. We'd drive the Jeep out to higher ground dripping wet; the dogs would either jump out to explore or a tired wet dog would jump in and shake off, eliciting a growl from Frank. He'd glance at me with a bemused smile as I dodged the spray.

I was the gate man, meaning I had to open all the gates. He'd smile, calling out to no one in particular, "Gate man…gate man," as he rolled up to a stop. It was a lagniappe, an unexpected joy for a healing young man. I was as happy as the dogs. It was awesome.

On one hot early June day, soon after I got to the ranch, our routine was interrupted. Frank drove me through a gate on the dike just near the house. When I got back in the seat, he said, "Boy, let's me and you go over to that oak and have a little talk." He let the clutch out. We slowly moved toward the shadow of an oak near the corner of an orange grove where the expansive pasture spread out to the left. The shade was pleasant. The distance couldn't have been more than forty yards from the dike but it felt much longer as I stiffened in my seat.

Now I had heard tales about stepfathers. I just knew, as they used to say in Kentucky corn fields, I was about to be "pulled outta the shuck." I swallowed hard, experiencing more than a little anxiety. Had I inadvertently transgressed some law or rule? I didn't think so but who knew? His eyes didn't give any hint of his feelings. My impression was that I was being called into the principal's office, yet it was out of character from what little I'd learned about him the last several days. If anything, I had begun to trust him. Now, at this sudden change, it was like a building thunderhead in my mind. I was uneasy.

He pulled the green Jeep up under that oak, cut the motor, and we sat a few minutes in silence. Mild pleasant smoke from his panatela moved in little eddies through the Jeep. He pushed his sweat-stained Stetson back a little removing the shadow from his face, and then draped his hands over the steering wheel. Every now and then, as was a habit, he'd roll his wedding band with his thumb and little finger. He took a deep breath, let it out slowly and began a life-changing conversation.

"Boy…, do you know why I married your mother?" The words hung in the air. It was getting awfully hot and stuffy for the middle of the morning. A bead of sweat trickled down my spine—the finger of dread? I had no idea where we were going in this conversation. I would have been content to let him do the talking. Silence…. It became obvious that he expected an answer. My pulse was racing. I really didn't have much to say. I could feel myself slipping into a defensive sullenness.

After an eternity I ventured an answer, "I guess you all love each other."

"That's exactly right." He said it without any hesitation. It was a somewhat soft but matter-of-fact statement, like a deacon verifying the total of offerings after a Sunday service.

After an uncomfortable pause, he continued, "Do you know I knew she had you when I asked her to marry me?" He looked at me for a moment when he asked it but glanced away to look out into the pasture. I guess he sensed my discomfort. What was he thinking? Where was this going?

"No," was my answer. A soft breeze came through the door of the Jeep, a few leaves on the oak rustled. A bee buzzed through the door of the Jeep on the way to work. She tried to find a way out through the windshield. He unconsciously waved a hand at her as if to say, "Move on…"

"Well, I did. She told me all about you. And because I love her, I love you. I am taking you as my son."

What did he just say? Were my ears hearing the words correctly? This wasn't anything like I thought it would be. Could I really trust this man? What was his motive? Why in the world would he take me under his care? I hadn't done anything to deserve it.

He continued, "I already have a son and a daughter. Sonny works here on the ranch. Sonny and Betty have three children, Kim, Wes and Karen. Biba and her husband Charles are in the Air Force. They come here in the summer. Her real name is Elizabeth, but we call her Biba. They have Susan and David."

There was a long pause. I could feel a little blowback heat off the engine in the light breeze. It popped a little as it cooled. I was awkwardly studying a marvelous seam on my shirttail. Smokey the Weimaraner jumped in the back of the Jeep. He sat there hassling from his run. He snapped at a biting fly. After a bit, he lay down with a low contented groan. His eyes were shut, but his ears were still working as he listened. But for me things were taking a sudden turn. This was not an ordinary situation; instead of criticism and verbal attacks, there was a germinating seed of encouragement.

Finally, after another puff on the panatela, he broke the silence. The ashes were about an inch and a half long by this time. He finally thumped the end of the cigar with his thumb. They fell harmlessly to the floor of the Jeep. I guess he was concentrating, too.

He said, "I have only one thing that I ask: Don't ever lie to me about anything. I can take a lot of things but I can't tolerate a liar. No matter how much it hurts, always tell the truth to me." To this I made a mental note but didn't respond. It was a reasonable request. This was his non-negotiable rule.

There was another long silence, as Frank puffed the cigar and refolded his hands on the steering wheel. Again, he looked out past the oak toward the back fence of the nearby orange grove. Then taking out a white handkerchief, still holding the panatela between the first two fingers of the left hand, he wiped the inside brim of the stained Stetson. His hair was matted from sweat. After removing his sunglasses, he wiped his forehead. I was busy making sure my fingernails were in order, since the shirttail seam was fine. Once he replaced his glasses and hat, he quietly asked, "You have any plans for the future?"

I was still thinking of the things he'd just said. I managed to rein in my runaway thoughts to answer, "Well…I guess I'll go into the Air Force…I passed the admission test. They want me to join."

He pondered that and said, "Why don't you take some time off and take a vacation before you do that. You have worked hard so you deserve a little time off. You can do anything you want to – you can sleep late, work here on the ranch or sit on your butt if you want. If you want to go on into the service after a summer off, that's fine. If you want to go to college, we can help you go. I don't see any problems with you doin' that. The ranch is set up so that all the kids can go to college if they want to. "

This was followed by another long silence and sounds of my shifting in the seat. Finally, I said, "Well, if you don't mind, I think I will take some time off, maybe until fall, then go into the Air Force."

With his slight nod, we agreed. So there it was. I had four options: sleep late and sit on my butt, work on the ranch, go to college someday, or enlist in the military. I had no idea what a significant change had just occurred in my life. Were these alternatives just talk or was he serious? Would I be able to work here? Could I even do the things they were doing on the ranch? I knew about some farm animals, but these wild cattle were different. To use a Texas phrase, "They'd eat your sack lunch!" What would it be like to be re-established in a family? Many questions came up in my mind. I took a deep breath and relaxed a little as we started up and headed for home. Let's play this out, seeing if what he said holds true. What did I have to lose? I didn't really know much about trust, but could I take advantage of this opportunity and unearned generosity? Was he serious about college? Who knew? I needed someone to trust and, too, someone to trust me. Was he the one?

He reached for the key, unconsciously saying, "Uh-huh", which was his way of signaling we were settled about it. He started the Jeep for home. Home…an odd but pleasant concept to me at the time. We didn't say anything on the way. My mother must have known that he was going to have a talk with me. She looked at him with unspoken appreciation for what he'd just done. It felt like a tremendous burden had been lifted, like chains had been cut away, freeing me.

I was intrigued. What kind of man was he? What made him tick? Was it environment, or the times? Was his character the product of inherited temperament or family up-bringing? I didn't know it at the time, but I had just begun a new life that would end with my becoming a veterinarian in an astonishing land and culture…in the very heart of Florida Cracker cowboy country.

Like a tide that stops rising and ebbs, things were changing. The wind was shifting. Currents were forming in channels unseen. My little ship would soon alter its course.

About His Early Days in Florida

"Our character is but the stamp on our souls of the free choices of good and evil we have made through our lives."
-John Cunningham Geikie

FRANK Wesley Williamson, Sr. was very good at seeing things as they could be, rather than as they were. I have no idea of the number of people he helped behind the scenes. I can name several that owe their education to him. I am one of them. He was embarrassed when people would thank him for the help. He'd shrug it off like it was a part of a bigger plan. Most of them have paid him back, some could not. It didn't matter to him either way. He advised, "Cast a little bread on the waters, but look downstream to see who gets it." I told him once that I would never be able to pay him back for all that he had done for me. He said he didn't expect it. He said, "When you get a chance, just pass it on."

He was born in Ohio in October of 1902, at the very start of the century. The family moved to Clearwater, Florida, while he was young. I never knew if the Williamson family came from the Cavalier or the Puritan-Separatist side of England, nor do I know if the original family was Saxon or infiltrated with Norman blood. The family, like thousands before them, probably came too late to get good land in Virginia or New England, and moved to a better life in Ohio. What prompted his daddy to move the family to Clearwater is not known. His mother's maiden name was Bouvier. She spoke fluent French. His daddy was a schoolteacher and principal of the one room school there at the time. I think his mother was a teacher as well. They spoke French at the dinner table when they wanted to have private remarks between them. The children knew basic table-item French, but never learned it conversationally.

He had a sister, Dorothy, whom we all called, "Sister". One day he was de-worming some bird dog puppies and Sister, not much more than a toddler, came out to watch. He said she looked a little wormy to him so he grabbed her and poked a piperazine dog-wormer capsule down her. He said, "Well, about two weeks later she slicked off and started gaining weight. I never told Mama about it." Sister owned The Highlander Restaurant in Lake Wales, Florida, many years later. The restaurant had several large glass display cages filled with colorful finches. They were fascinating to watch while enjoying your meal. He told her, when we ate there, "You have too many things on the menu…I don't think you can make everything well. Why don't you specialize in a few excellent things?" Both were being stubborn about it. She'd ignore his suggestions.

Frank said his daddy's first day at the new school was a lesson in boxing. He got the class together and asked for someone to volunteer. The biggest bully in the whole school volunteered, of course. He made a serious mistake. "Daddy" Williamson cleaned his plow, as has been aptly said. He never had a problem with discipline from that day on.

He had a business also. I recall it's having something to do with construction. One of his employees, a black man, had the strength to carry two one hundred-pound sacks of cement mix out in front of his body. He was over 6 feet tall and solid muscle. Everybody figures that all black folks were mistreated in those days. Frank said his daddy told him to "Take care of the men", just before he died. He would frequently go by the houses of the retired men (which, incidentally, his daddy had given them) and checked on them, taking them to the doctor or bringing them groceries or game occasionally. He did this until they all died of old age.

Frank was remarkably self-sufficient from an early age. He was about twelve years old when, on Friday afternoons, he'd come home from school, get his hunting gear and some personal items together and pull out for the woods. It wasn't much of a walk to the edge of town and the wilderness. He'd not come in until Sunday evening. All weekend he'd be alone in the woods. "Mother and Daddy didn't question me. They let me do as I pleased…" he said. Hunting was a way of life. He'd take three to six shotgun shells (that was all he needed) and kill a squirrel the first thing. He'd put on a slow-cooking Dutch oven of squirrel and rice pilau, he pronounced "perlue" as the Crackers called it. He'd cover the top of the oven with red coals, letting it slow-cook for the hours while he hunted. When he'd come back to camp after dark, his meal would be ready. A favorite meal was big yellow lima beans. He'd take a quart jar of his mama's cooked beans to the woods on occasion.

In his twenties Frank was a professional bird hunter and contracted to supply quail for the hotels in Clearwater and Tampa. Game was plentiful in pioneer times in Florida. He said the best year he ever had was a quail count of some 1500 birds. At that time, he hunted with an English Pointer named Jack. Jack had a dark liver spot over one eye. Robert Butler, the artist, then in his early twenties, painted a picture of him from an old photo. Jack had a habit of rolling his eyes back at you if you missed a shot, as if to say, "Now what was that all about?" He said Jack was an absolutely perfect bird dog. A Field and Stream photographer brought a motion picture camera down to capture him in action. I don't know if anyone knows if the film still is in existence. This annual quail harvest didn't put even a dent in population since there were thousands and thousands more. Later, the tourists did, by moving into areas where the birds once thrived. The biggest threat for bird dogs in those days was rattle snakes and water moccasins.

This habit of slipping off into the woods to hunt and camp continued for most of his life, though later he'd drive a vehicle. Frank talked of hunting with Marjorie Kinnan Rawlings, the Pulitzer Prize winning author of *The Yearling, Golden Apples, Cross Creek, South Moon Under* and a few other books. He said she could hunt like the men but was an alcoholic, writing some of her works while under the influence. He used to go up to the swamps around Cross City, Florida, where he sometimes hunted with a man named Henry Cannon. Henry had an uncanny, almost mystical woodsman's sense. He was highly intelligent, but had no formal education. Frank would make a trip back into the woods, arriving late. It wouldn't be long before Henry would show up to drink coffee. He asked him, "How did you know I'd be here tonight? I didn't know myself till about dark that I was comin'." Henry would say, "I jus' had a feelin'." He just knew it. Henry could tell you almost exactly where a buck-deer would go when the dogs picked up his scent. Frank told me that he knew people who were like that in the woods. They "just knew" things that could have not been known by normal means.

Boats from Central America and Cuba would unload their cargos of bananas at the Tampa docks and young Frank would buy some near-ripe bunches. He'd hang them in a shade oak in the town square and put up a sign reading, "Bananas – 5 cents a bunch." He'd supply a knife and cigar box nearby and people would cut off all they wanted and leave the money. He expanded his "fast food" business by selling fried squirrel to the winter bicyclers. One time there was a problem with one group; they'd eat the entire batch of fried squirrel and not leave any money. When they did this a couple of days straight, he figured out the best way to stop it. He killed a mess of rats from under the feed store, skinned them, cleaned them all up and fried them out back of the house. He said he was afraid his mama would jump on him, "like a duck on a June bug", if she'd known what he planned. The next day, the bait of fried rats disappeared from the basket just as the squirrels had. The young supplier left a note: "I appreciate you all helping me clean out the rats from the feed store." There was never a problem with paying for the fried squirrel from that point on.

He slyly admitted that as a boy he occasionally stole a chicken "for a pilau," no doubt. He detailed for me the technique of stealing a chicken from its roost. In total darkness, he explained, you had to quietly and gently ease a wrist or forearm under the bird. He'd ease the head under a wing and clamp the bird under his arm. He said if it was properly done, not a chicken in the hen house would stir. According to him it was a skill few folks mastered. He got caught once, I think. He had to return it. But his idea was to put the stolen bird back on the roost, leaving her as if it had been for her a bad dream. I got the impression the owner of the coop knew the kids occasionally did this as well as borrow a few watermelons. I guess the man thought it was just a cost of doing business.

Somewhere around this time, Frank made a deal with a man in Clearwater. The man would give him ten acres if he would clear another ten acres for him. He set to it and went to work, digging out the roots of pine stumps. He built huge fires to get rid of the roots and tended the fires for days. He carried quarts of rice and big yellow lima beans to the site. (He never lost his liking of them. His mama would fix them whenever he said his "taster called for them".) Often he carried a pot and dry rice. Adding a squirrel or two to it he made a perlue. He'd stay there in heat, rain storms, mosquitoes, gnats and sun. He'd dig down around the massive stumps of the cut virgin pine trees, setting fires with literd to burn them out. Apparently, his parents didn't worry about him. He said the work was brutal--and that was probably a vast understatement.

Just about the time he was finishing up the man's ten acres while planning to begin clearing his ten acres, a surveyor came by, asking who owned the property around the area, including the ten acres that now belonged to Frank. He convinced the surveyor to run Highway 19 north of Clearwater right through the middle of his untouched ten acres. He could point out all the good reasons for doing something. He had a knack of making you see things his way, and all the time you knew he was getting the best end of the trade but somehow it didn't matter, because you got a good deal, too.

I think this was the way he accumulated the capital for his other ventures. There's no telling what that property would be worth today. I've purposely driven the route down Highway 19 to Clearwater. You'd never think it was wilderness at one time.

From bananas, chicken stealing, fried squirrels (and rats), the sale of property, professional quail hunting, feed store owner, and plant nursery-man, he went on to vegetable growing in the Everglades, ranching, planting citrus groves, citrus care-taking, catfish farming, setting up a catfish process-ing plant, and for a time, soybean farming. He just had a knack for making things work. He saw potential where others walked on by. When developing the ranch in Okeechobee a few of the old timers said he was crazy to think of draining the marshes at the ranch. "Everybody knows that land is lower than Lake Okeechobee. A ditch will bring water in from the lake." He studied the old surveyor's maps and knew that the property there was considerably higher than the lake. I think he said it was higher by 14 feet or so. People were astounded when the final cut was made and water flowed out, not in!

Frank did the same thoughtful planning about citrus groves. He fig-ured on it a long time, probably on many of those lonely Jeep rides. He fi-nally told Sonny that he was sure that oranges could be grown in Okeecho-bee County. If they could raise them in the Indian River area, they could do it there. He designed and installed a bed and ditch system that solved the problems of water control. He liked making grove irrigation systems. Long runs of concrete pipes were laid in ditches then covered with dirt. Big con-crete water-diversion boxes with outgoing pipes to run water to every part of the grove were added. All one had to do was lay a board against the open-ing of the section that you wanted to shut off. The water pressure would hold the board in place while water was diverted into the desired pipe. Once while making these concrete boxes, he lost in the cement his first wedding band that my mother gave him. Mama got him another. Somewhere in the First Grove, cast in solid concrete, rests a gold wedding ring. It has been there over 45 years now. Many years later she gave me his second one. I have it on.

It soon became apparent that I was in the company of a unique indi-vidual. On the trips in the Jeep, he'd sometimes get on a tear, talking non-stop. I wanted to know about everything. Perhaps he was healing, too. I was somewhat in awe of the fact that he took me as I was, a big bruised kid, lack-ing confidence, direction and goals. So my first June in this new world was a time of many adjustments. It didn't take long for me to recognize I really did need, in the truest sense of the word, to take some time off before entering the Air Force. I awkwardly asked if I could work a little on the ranch. Frank was in the home office when I approached him. He stopped his book work, leaned back in the leather chair and studied my face a little, with a gentle smile. Could he have sensed I was a little anxious about approaching him? He finally said, "Boy, I think it'd do you some good. It's fine with me...I'll talk to Sonny." He then told me to go to town and get a hat, boots and gloves. He said, "If you're gonna work you'll need them. Cow huntin' is comin' up next month. Just tell 'em to charge it to me." Cow huntin'? What in the world was that?

After our talk, I remember the first Jeep ride to town by myself to purchase these necessities. Yes, at 45 miles per hour it belched black clouds like a Navy destroyer laying down a smoke screen. I parked on the wide oak-lined main street and went into the ranch supply store, Merserve's Hardware. The Merserve family had been in Okeechobee for generations. I wandered in, enveloped by the smells of leather, disinfectant, long-shelved items and many unidentifiable things. A pale-complexioned man in a short sleeved western shirt with pointed yoke and snap-buttons, blue jeans and cowboy boots approached and asked, "Whut can we do for ya'?" I told him what I needed and he first took me over to the gloves, where I selected a soft tough pair of goat skin gloves that fit well. Next stop was the knife display where I picked out a yellow handled three-bladed pocket knife, like the cowboys carried. I asked where I could get some boots and a hat and was told to go around the corner to the western wear store. He quoted the total for the two items. I did as instructed, telling the man at the cash register to charge the bill to Frank Williamson, adding, "He said it would be okay." The man looked a little confused, glanced sharply at me and asked, "Who are you?" I told him I was his stepson. Well, the whole atmosphere changed, like a brilliant dawning. He wanted to know all about when I came there, where I was from and other juicy tidbits. All hot items for gossip, no doubt. I didn't say much but he appeared delighted. There was no hesitation in charging the bill. I didn't even have to sign the ticket. I had never had the experience of walking into a place of complete strangers and being accepted because of the mere mention of a name. Around the corner I found the western wear store, picked out work boots, a good straw cowboy hat and a couple pairs of Levis. The same thing happened when I told him to charge it to Frank Williamson. No problem...though they didn't know me from Adam's house cat, they knew him and that was enough. This was my first introduction to the tremendous advantage of a good reputation.

The Cracker cowboys would say about wealthy people, "You can just smell the money on them." But I noticed that many of those that had an abundance of material goods were fundamentally unhappy. They had a general defensiveness about them. I expect it was the constant barrage of people trying to get in their pockets, trying to sell them something that made them suspicious. And, too, when people respect you for your wealth, you could easily begin to believe that you're truly exceptional because of it. Next thing you know, you're focused on attaching your self-worth to money.

I could see no sign that Frank had ever fallen into this trap. He was the same everyday with everyone. He wore the same modest western clothes, clean and neat. You would never know he was a rich man, He never defended, hoarded or protected. His business philosophy was, "Always allow the other men to make a nickel off the deal." He sometimes loaned money where he had an idea he'd never get it back. He took the attitude that if he was not paid back, it was their problem—not his. I suspect that he figured if someone owed him money, he wouldn't be seeing them anytime soon and that was not an unwanted situation. My mama was the opposite. She had an ingrained sacrosanct ethic that you kept your word and paid your debts. Consequently, she was unforgiving of those who abused loans – especially those made by her husband. He'd quietly admonish her, "Let it go, Reeda." She'd fuss and fume for a while and eventually do as he suggested.

I've never known anyone as generous as he was, who handled wealth as well as he, thinking that it was only good if you could help somebody. His attitude was that it was all a gift and that generosity was expected from those to whom God had given much. This was a major part of his character. Ben Franklin reportedly said, "The greatest invention of man is compounded interest." Frank believed that living debt-free and thus contented was the greatest thing. Another business philosophy of his: "Have more than one way to pay off loans." His reputation was such that on several occasions he called Rupert Mock, his banker in Pahokee, who, on Frank's word alone, put five- or six-figure funds into his account, no paperwork, no handshake, no questions, no signature, no nothing, just a quiet, brief phone call. How long does it take to develop that kind of reputation?

The experience of the hardware and western wear stores taught me a life lesson. A good reputation is earned, not bought. I have thought about this and, in retrospect, believe then and there I began to see the importance of a good one. No one questioned him or his family.

It dawned on me in the months that followed that he was willing to dismiss my past deficiencies, my future difficulties, and to wait for his consistent guidance and patience to take hold. What was potentially another verse of the same song of my early life was rapidly changing. It was like a sunrise in my soul; then and there I guessed I was about as fortunate as anyone can be; I must never take him for granted, never disappoint him, if I could possibly help it, and love him back in the same way he loved me, unconditionally. Reverberating around in the back of my mind was a soft melody that was new to me.

The Ranch Crew

Crackers are a "soft-voiced, easy-going, childlike kind of folk, quick to anger, vindictive when their rage is protracted and becomes a feud; and generous and noble in their rough hospitality. But they live the most undesirable of lives, and surrounded by every facility for a luxurious existence, subsist on hog and hominy, and drink the meanest whiskey."
-Quote of Edward King, in *Oranges and Alligators: Sketches of South Florida Life*, By Iza Duffus Hardy

FRANK WESLEY WILLIAMSON, JR., nicknamed "Sonny", was my second introduction to character, after his daddy. He was slim, wiry-tough, the same deep lines in his face as his father, with a pleasant way about him. I felt he understood and perhaps identified with me some, having similar experiences from the split of his mother and daddy many years before. I'll never know if his daddy had a talk with him, but he cut me a lot of slack.

We naturally enjoyed each other's company. He was some 12 years older than I was, but had just enough boy left in him to pull pranks on me from the very beginning. I recollect one particular time when he and Betty went out to dinner with us to an upscale seafood restaurant in Ft Pierce. We unloaded from the car and while heading to the entrance he grabbed my elbow and began shaking my left forearm as if I were in a spasm, very similar to a person with palsy. In a mock tone of sympathy, he said loudly, "Come on, Howard…you can do it…" Mama looked back at us, probably embarrassed at our antics, because she said, "Y'all stop…" Frank just smirked. Sonny and I grinned like two otters that had just found a jar of peanut butter.

Sonny loved to fly more than anyone I'd ever met. I guess that is why he took the J-3 Cub up for any legitimate reason, like obtaining tractor parts, but some of the flights had pretty lame excuses. On more than one occasion he buzzed me on a tractor or in some vehicle. You really couldn't hear him coming at first. He'd line me up from behind, backing off the throttle a bit to lose altitude and open it wide open as he went over. By the time you knew you were buzzed, whatever you were driving rumbled and vibrated and you were looking up at the tailed underbelly of the bright yellow machine. He also loved running the airboat in the swamps and marshes on frog gigging and gator hunting expeditions. He later mentioned that he had been rejected for military pilot's training because a radiological "spot on a lung." It was bad enough to keep him out of pilot's training but didn't hamper anything else. A partial lobectomy had been performed sometime after the diagnosis. It was apparently an old benign, encapsulated tuberculosis nodule. He was fine, but I still think he would have given his eye teeth to fly in WW II.

After his graduation from the University of Florida in 1950, he and Miss Betty Chandler were married in Okeechobee. Following one year in Ft Lauderdale, where he was a construction bulldozer operator, they returned to become an integral part of the ranch. By the time he and I became acquainted, he had a solid nine years first-hand experience in developing the operation. During this time he'd worked as tractor, bulldozer and dragline operator and mechanic, in pasture development, as cowboy and foreman of a cow crew, and citrus grove design, tree planting and caretaking. He had ground-level knowledge of what it took to develop, run and maintain an agricultural enterprise. There comes a time when a man in such a diverse endeavor becomes more valuable in management than in trying to do all aspects of the work himself. Sonny was at this point in his life. He was making the transition from laborer to manager, using first-hand experience as his foundation. Nevertheless, he still enjoyed a good day's work in a saddle, taking apart a broken tractor, welding or otherwise getting his hands dirty repairing a dozer. He was a genius at mechanical repairs and innovation.

At first we had some difficulty in agreeing on a name we both could use for his daddy and my stepfather. I was uncomfortable calling my him by his first name, although he wouldn't have given a tinker's dam what I called him. "Daddy" was a little uncomfortable as well, although I used it with Sonny and Biba some. I also called him "Granddaddy" with some of the grand children. Over the course of that summer, we kind of settled on a name for our mutual father: "Paw." Sonny and I called him "Pappy" some, but we accepted "Paw" as a name we could both use and Paw didn't mind. When I write about him I still interchange "Paw" and "Frank".

And then there was the issue of the name I was to be called. We both went by the nickname "Sonny." We were both "Jr.'s", but he was there first, so I was stuck with my given name, which Sonny exaggerated, "How-Word."

He enjoyed the same things I did. He was quick to laugh, finding humor in the same places I found it. We would both laugh at something like, "I'd rather have a bottle in front-of-me, than have a frontal lobotomy". He could follow things to their logical conclusion, but then he'd make a leap into some outlandish hilariously dry comment. Irony was great sport to him. He was athletic, quick-witted, and intelligent. He really was a blessing as step-brothers go.

Sonny was what I later called an "analytical contrarianist," meaning he would take an opposing position purely for the stimulating conversation it would provoke. He'd get this twinkle in his eyes, a little smirk, and then plow into the debate with a zinger comment, just to see what we'd say. Kim, his older daughter, the attorney, has this ability, too. More than a few times, he forced me to consider other options. He had the knack of reducing arguments to a basic, absurd syllogism – the technique is sometimes called, *reductio ad absurdum*. This only means that he reduced false arguments to their logical absurdity or as a Cracker might say it, "Put hair in the cake." I, on the other hand was *reductio ad absurdum ad infinitum ad nauseum*. Paw summed it up as, "Boy, you're gaggin' on gnats agin."

Sonny sometimes quoted his friend Robert Arnold when we were finished with a group of calves. In fact, he quoted the phrase when something was pleasing. Robert, as best I know, was from the Arnold pioneer Cracker family in the Okeechobee area. He was a little tongue-tied. What might have been a handicap to some was never an issue with the cowboys or people that knew him. In fact I never met anyone who didn't like him. When referring to something that was pleasant, he'd say, "Dat wuz dood to me – uh-huh." He'd use the comment in any context, from a good taste of guava cobbler, a good meal of beefsteak and stewed swamp cabbage, to a cool drink of water. Sonny modified the phrase to, "That was dood to 'im, wadn't it?"indicating that the object of his comment was pleased or refreshed. I never met Robert but met some of his kin. In fact DeRoy Arnold, who eventually worked on the ranch, pulled me out from under a mountain mare precariously balanced on three legs after a spill on ice in Montana. The mare slipped, I pushed off the saddle and we both went butt over tea kettle down a steep slope. I was able to latch on to a log buried in the snow. DeRoy came up beside me and started dragging me, which I thought was odd, until I looked up and saw the mare right above me! How I got out of that wreck with only a bad knee, I'll never understand.

But, I still use that phrase with affection, "Caus' it's dood to me, uh-huh!" never failing to think of Robert and DeRoy.

Sonny had more than a little devilment in him, no doubt inherited from his daddy. We started and ended the days there at the shop. Repairs took time, parts had to be waited on and delivered. I remember one occasion a disassembled International tractor transmission lay on the concrete floor in organized piles spread out like some mechanical jig-saw puzzle, a mass of shiny metallic gears, gaskets, bolts, nuts, tools and associated paraphernalia. Sonny's brother-in-law, Charles, was the ranch mechanic, a spit-and-polished, strictly-by-the-book ex-military organizer. One day Sonny said, "I wonder what would happen if there was a bolt left over when it was all put back together." I innocently followed him into the parts storage area where he carefully selected a bolt very close in design to the ones meticulously laid out in the shop. We tossed the extra bolt into a pile of similar hardware. Several days went by. Parts arrived, work began. As we observed Charles' mounting frustration, tight jaw becoming more and more pronounced, we chickened out. With a sheepish grin, Sonny 'fessed-up'. There was a nervous laugh of relief as I recall. We didn't try that again. I don't think he'll remember the episode. I do because I was guilty by association…

While I was learning that summer, Sonny was very patient with me until one day I messed up while gathering some bulls; it was irresponsibility on my part. We were saddled and moving when Sonny spoke to the crew, asking us to clear a pasture of a group of bulls, most of them being very lazy Herefords. Sonny said for us to especially watch out for the English bulls. He said, "They're bad to stop in the shade under a small cabbage palm an' just stay there like a fat man on a picnic. Y'all could ride right by a few and miss 'em, if you aren't careful."

The idea was to remove all bulls and restock the pasture with cows and calves. Leaving a bull could cause problems in the calving season. Some cows could be bred at an inappropriate time, ending up with a calf out of the planned birthing season. So it was important to not leave a bull in the pasture. Somehow, I don't recall how, I missed one. Sonny came out of the thick underbrush, exactly from the direction I thought I'd cleared, bringing a Hereford bull. He had found him under a cabbage palm rubbing his head on the palm fronds and switching his tail to keep the aggravating flies at bay. He brought him out without a word, joining the group. A hot pot of his temper boiled over on me. He verbally jerked a knot in my tail for the oversight, telling me that they depended on me to do what they asked. I believe that was the only time we had words. Maybe that's the reason I remember it. Sonny and I almost immediately healed our budding relationship. It was probably just a matter of a day or two before it was all forgotten. Looking back on it from the far side of experience it was a good incident. I learned something by my mistake. That's valuable.

HUBERT WALDRON was a rugged man, confident, knowledgeable, and capable to meet any threat. He was usually all business but dryly humorous. Hubert was reared in Indian Town, Florida, where His daddy was the sheriff. Hubert told me that one of his childhood chores was driving the Model T to the front of jook joints while his daddy waited in the back. (A jook was Cracker slang for a honkey tonk, dance hall, or road house. A "headskin" is the synonym for a jook but leaned toward meaning, "a place where there were frequent fights".) He said there would be the "Clang" of a shovel on something hard and his daddy would drag some unconscious criminal around front for the trip to the jail. When you broke the law in Indian Town, punishment started upon resisting arrest. There are stories of men in the area that were wanted for a killing, often in fair fights or in self-defense. It was told that word was sent to some men to turn themselves in. One man reportedly said, "Go on back. I'll be along in a day or two." Sure enough he showed up a day or two later at the sheriff's office. That was a whole lot better alternative than a shovel to the head, I reckon.

Hubert had worked on the ranch a few years by the time I first met him. His hands were rough and calloused, his face weather-beaten. He was stocky, even a little overweight, but under that layer of fat was pure muscle. He was reserved around new people, requiring time to get to know them. Reminding me of a cur dog when a stranger came up, he would look cautiously at them, waiting to see what they wanted. In fact, he was rather quiet around me at first. He could be as ornery as a rattlesnake, borderline mean when the situation called for it, and was tougher than the bark on an oak tree, yet he was as gentle with an orphan calf as a sweet grandmother with her newborn grandson. I don't recall many times when he didn't remove his hat when my mother came around. He was protective of helpless creatures, like calves and innocent children and women. He was a man under self-control—most of the time. However, you didn't want to light his fuse, so to speak. His two brothers, Curtis and Clifford, were cast from the same mold.

Hubert told of a time when Curtis stopped by the house at twilight. Curtis had on clean jeans, with his hair slicked down. He was the ranch manager for the Acree Ranch, at the time, across Highway 441. As they visited about different things a rifle shot rang out in the distance popping like a can of store-bought biscuits, echoing in the woods near the horse barn. Immediately Curtis knew it was the turkey hunter he'd been trying to catch on the Acree property and he figured the man was slipping into a hammock where the turkeys frequently roosted. Curtis told Hubert to load up in the truck and they took off with Hubert still holding Reeny, his 2 year old daughter.

Off they raced toward the hammock. They spotted the man's truck lights as he headed toward Okeechobee. The race was on, Curtis with jaw set to run the fella down and Hubert holding on to the baby. They followed him to his home, getting there as he stepped up on his porch. He turned to see Curtis coming around the front of his truck. "Whut do you want?"

"You're the one who's been trespassing on private land and illegally huntin' Mr. Acree's turkeys. I'm here for the turkey. That's Mr. Acree's turkey." He thrust a thick calloused finger at the bird.

The man eyed him, grumbling some off-colored remark about Curtis's lineage and that he was asking for trouble. Curtis told him that he was not leaving until he got the turkey. Well the situation escalated to the point that the man pretty much threw down the gauntlet, saying that Curtis might be asking for a whippin'. Curtis told him to step down into the yard and they would settle it right then and there. Well, the fella underestimated his visitors.

Like two mean scrub bulls they went at it tooth and nail in the dew-wetted grass of the man's front yard. Curtis was wearing house slippers as is the custom for many working men and women after they'd had a long day. When Curtis would shift his weight to rotate his hips to "carry the mail", as he called it, in his punch, his right foot would slip. Hubert said it sounded like someone slapping a beef carcass with a baseball bat. Back and forth they traded punches. The noise and clamor was causing baby Reeny to cry in Hubert's arms. He said, "I saw his feet slippin' in those house shoes and knew he wadn't gettin' traction…I told him, 'Come here, Curtis, hold this baby and let me have a go at 'im'." After a furious time of meat-slapping, grunts, a couple of puffy eyes and lips, and a frustrated Hubert holding a screaming baby, the man held up his hands saying, "Okay…okay…take the (*expletive deleted*) turkey. I've had enough." Curtis walked over, took the turkey from the porch, and blurted, "You comin' back?" The man replied as he held a hand to his jaw, "Naw, man…"

One warm day, right after I met Hubert and before I had started working, I was enjoying the swimming pool beside the house. It was fed by an artesian well and the water was colder than kraut. Hubert and a crew were moving some cattle in order to prepare for cow hunting the next month. A big heifer broke loose from the herd and made a beeline toward the pasture behind the house. She came by the pool and, for some reason, climbed the steps and ran off into the water. I was standing on the diving board, lily-white in my swim suit, looking like a skinny pond bird watching an alligator. I was trying to decide the best escape route, though I was pretty sure she'd not try the board. Hubert rode up with his rope uncoiled, ready for action. He grinned at me and yelled at the heifer, trying to force her out of the pool. She swam around, finally found the steps, climbed out and circled to the far edge. Hubert got off his horse, went up to the big deck at the shallow end and boogered her with his hat. She lowered her head and started for him, but her hooves wouldn't grab traction. They shot out behind her every time she tried to butt him. He laughed out loud. She gave up, jumped down to the lawn and pulled out for the herd. He never said a word to me. He saddled up and left.

I call to mind Hubert's getting frothing mad at a man who spoke disrespectfully to Mr. Frank. He grabbed me by the arm, pushed me toward the Jeep, saying, "Stepandfetchit, git me outta here before I gut-shoot that son of a (*colorful language questioning heritage deleted*)." I learned a new phrase that day from Hubert – not *the deleted expletive*, but "gut shoot". "Gut shooting" was a terrible way to die. I treated a few animals that had been gut shot and it was not a pleasant experience. That was the worst thing Hubert could think of, I guess. I had already learned "son of a (*colorful language questioning heritage deleted*)" as a young boy in Kentucky. Hubert got the "Stepandfetchit" name from Paw. I suspect it originated with the black actor so named in the Will Rogers movies. It fit me. Come to think of it, that was what I was good at. I had a natural talent for fetching. I was also referred to as "Whistle-britches." I guess that came from the old corduroy pants legs that rubbed together when you walked.

Hubert once told me, "The ol' man never used to talk much." Somehow, "the ol' man" wasn't derogatory coming from Hubert. It was more a term of respect. He went on to tell me that Mr. Frank appeared to be a lonely man, saying, "He'd talk to ya if you asked him something. He'd ride that Jeep everywhere on the ranch, looking at everything. He'd go off several days, then one day he'd be back prowlin' around." He added, "He opened up when your mama came along. He'll talk to you now, but there was a time that he didn't say much." I had little knowledge of the reasons for the loneliness that happened before my time. I gathered from bits and pieces of conversations that Frank had disastrous past relationships with women. By the time I knew him, he'd healed considerably, putting all of that behind him, accepting them as part of his life experiences. There was no spite, resentment or regret that I could detect. He'd let it all go. He was at peace with my mother. That's all I cared about, that someone loved my bruised mother. But was he still healing, too? Funny how we three bruised souls united...

Frank at times would stop the Jeep out a ways from the activities, watching for long minutes or hours, Hubert dig with the dragline. Hubert could cast the bucket of the orange monster to within six-inches of his target, draw it back, load it with sand or muck, then rotate the boom over to a dumping site. He'd release the bucket to drop its load and rotate back, casting the bucket again. This went on and on hypnotically. The whole area smelled of wet, musty dirt, sometimes sour from the fermented vegetation. The dogs loved to roll in the fresh sand or lie on their bellies to cool off. Hubert was skilled in heavy equipment operation like bulldozers and road graders. That was when the ranch was in development. They dug canals to drain marshes and control water, hollowed out watering ponds for cattle and wildlife and planted groves and pastures.

When Hubert would take a break from the tedious repetition (unusual for him), Mr. Frank would comment, "Kinda hard runnin' that dragline and keeping the mosquitoes out your nose, ain't it?" Hubert, who was not afraid of anything, was a little in awe of him. This was a time when people were more loyal to their employers and good jobs could be scarce.

In the early days I had no hint of the influence for good Hubert would have on me. He never let me shortcut anything; you had to finish the job—always. He never looked at a watch or a clock and I didn't either when we worked together. He would chuckle deeply as I described a fall from a horse or some other wreck I'd had. He enjoyed and encouraged my increasing confidence. He had his faults like us all, but he loved his wife and children and he had a highly developed sense of loyalty. He could be gentle as a lamb or meaner than a snake. He took me under his wing. I liked him and he liked me.

Hubert, in one of his joking moods, responded to a man who complained about his wife, "Yeah…a man sure pays dearly for what little lovin' he gets…" I can still hear his quiet laughter.

HARRIS SILLS, whom we called "Partner," was from West Florida, up in the Panhandle area. He sired, I think, nineteen kids. I never knew Mrs. Sills well. The times I went to pick up Partner, she didn't say much, not looking too friendly toward strangers, a characteristic of many Crackers. I only met a few of his children. Many had left home early to pursue their own activities. We didn't cross paths much.

He had been at Caloosa Ranch since it was founded around 1941. His first job, which he considered a total waste of time, was planting pine trees along the road coming from the highway. He did it, but he didn't like it. Why plant trees next to a road when there were so many around? If you waited long enough, wouldn't the myrtle bushes take the roadside? I guess this "tree plantin' bidness" was like being in the Army to Partner: Dig this hole so the next platoon can fill it up. ...

Paw said that he was a powerful man when he was in his prime and the best calf catcher around. One time, during branding, he picked out the biggest calf in the pen and grabbed his back leg. The calf shook him so hard that his false teeth rattled. We laughed when someone told that story. I first knew him in his fifties, but you could tell that at one time he'd had a big chest and strong forearms. A calf could kick the fire out of him and he would only say something like, "Why, I wish you look at that, he kicked me so hard both brogans come untied." Partner was renowned for understatement. One time we were working in the groves, hoeing orange tree re-sets, replacing the dead or diseased trees. The sun was murder that day. Down in between the trees where we worked there was no air moving. You could get "bear caught" there. "Bear caught" meant heat stroke or exhaustion. I was seeing everything through a yellow haze. Partner stopped, took off his hat and wiped his shiny white forehead with an old pocket rag saying, "I guess we mite git hot here in a little while." Somehow the understatement struck me as funny in spite of my near-coma.

As I said, Partner sired nineteen kids. Along about child number 15 or 16 the men discussed it with him. "Partner, are y'all ever gonna quit havin' kids?" and "Boy, I'd hate to hav' yer grocery bill." They asked Sonny what he would recommend. He came up with what we thought was a workable plan to help him prevent additional births, a crude birth control method, as it were. The men elbowed each other, smirking as they watched Partner's face while Sonny explained it to him. According to Sonny's plan, Partner was to take orange juice when he got the urge to procreate. Well, as nature continuously moves, in the spring, Partner announced that his wife was pregnant again. In mock amazement, everyone dryly commented that they couldn't see how this could happen since, as they told it, "Sonny's plan looked foolproof." After thoughtful reflection, Sonny said, "Partner, I think there's been a misunderstanding, I meant you were to drink orange juice 'instead of', not 'with'." Partner pushed his straw cowboy hat up on his head and with a twinkle in his eye, said, "I 'spect so."

I remember going out on the ranch to places that were thick and wild, riding alone, exploring with the dogs. I'd imagine I was the first white man to ever see such remote places. Then I would spy a rusty can of Beanie Weenies. Partner ate a can of them for lunch every day. We asked him why he ate so many cans of these beans and he said they kept the gas off his stomach. He hardly ever trimmed his fingernails. We never knew why, but he reasoned that he might need them to pick up a dollar bill. He was a teller of tall tales.

Of all the characters I would get to know, Partner stands out as one of the most memorable. After the initial introduction and later working closely with him, I found Partner was overflowing with dry Cracker humor. In fact, I would say he was foundational in my appreciation of it. As we worked together he delighted in telling me stories and tall tales. One day he went into a detailed description of what it was like to swallow a "gallonnipper," referring to a large species of mosquito, named for the volume of blood she could suck. We found a shed rattlesnake skin in one of the groves once. He claimed that a "gallonipper got 'im an' sucked 'im bone-dry…" He then went on to explain how this one particular mosquito he had swallowed caught hold of his esophagus midway down. He said, "It feels kinda like a small cat holding on in ther'…" He described how the mosquito was trying to crawl back up his throat. He graphically demonstrated how he had to keep swallowing to hold her down. The more I watched him the funnier it became. Somehow we did manage to get a large amount of work done.

He told about the time he was riding up to Kissimmee on a wagon. He said, "Well sir, jus before I got to tha Osceola County line, I seen this man walkin' south with palmetto fans in each hand. He wuz swinging real wild at the mosquitoes that wuz all clouded around him." He demonstrated how the man was frantically swatting the clouds of pests off his back, chest and face. Partner said, "I spoke to the fella and said, 'These mosquitoes are bad, ain't they?'" Partner grinned and said the man replied, "Yeah, but wait till you git to Osceola County, they're hell up there!"

By this time I began to get the idea that he was partial to mosquito stories. He told of the time that he and several men were on a hunting trip in the Big Cypress Swamp. He said, "Well, dark came an' we all bedded down in a tent, since the mosquitoes wuz plum murder outside. You could jus' hear them whinin' out there in the night. Everyone slept purty good. I woke up a few times but it was still dark. We could hear the mosquitoes whinin' an' zoo-zooin' around outside. I tossed and turned some. I noticed that some of the others were restless, too. Finally, I just couldn't stay in the bedroll any longer. I thought I would git up and git ready for breakfast. Well, the next thing you know everyone was up. One was getting his clothes folded and stored while another was trying to shave in the dark tent by the light of a Coleman lantern. One man wuz cleanin' his shotgun. He didn't realize he had left a shell in the chamber and as he wiped the oil next to the trigger, it went off and blew a 12-inch hole in the top of the tent. The sun shined in -- it was 11:30 in the morning! Those mosquitoes had covered the tent 12 inches thick!"

On one boring hot day in the groves, Partner took off his hat and wiped his brow. "One time in West Florida" he started, "when I was a little tyke, I watched a fox come up to a creek wher I wuz fishin'. I crawled over behind some bushes to watch. He come up to the edge of the water and eased into it real slow like. I thought he sure wuz actin' funny so I kept watchin' him. Wellsir that fox waded in and lowered hisself down into the water real slow. Then he eased his whole body under water. Finally only his head was showin'. He lowered it real slow until only the tip of his nose wuz showin', then he went completely under, swum under water to the other bank. All that was left where he went under was a brown ball. I had no idee whut it wuz, sos I just went over and picked it up. It wuz a ball of fleas...Can you believe it?" (Of course I did...at first.)

Sonny told me one time that the men were rousting bulls out of a pasture when they approached a palmetto patch and spied a bobcat darting through, running from one little clump to another. The bobcat was being cautious in his escape. Sonny spotted the same cat several times. He turned to Partner and dryly asked, "Partner, how many bobcats do you think are in there?" Partner said, "Well, I've counted 27 so far." This was a typical comment from Partner.

You never knew when he'd come up with something. He told me one day he'd just witnessed a puzzlin' thing. Of course by this time I knew what was coming. He said he was working in the Grapefruit Grove and came upon a king snake and a rattler fighting under a tree. He said he watched the whole thing. He went into detail about how the king snake rocked from side to side, how the rattler sounded off with his characteristic rattling and how they sized each other up. After this animated description, he said, "Wellsir, tha rattler grabs the king snake's tail. The king snake grabs the rattler's tail and they commenced to eat each other. Slowly they worked up the bodies until finally, poof! They just disappeared! They jus' et each other up...." (What?)

On another hot, humid summer day, Partner and I were hoeing the weeds around replacement trees, what we called, "resets", planted where the sick or dead orange trees had been removed. The weeds would compete for the fertilizer so they had to be dug out to give the new trees a vigorous start in life. It had been a long day. We had been moving from row to row. Sore backs, tender arms and shoulder muscles, and fatigue were taking a toll. The intense afternoon sun beat down on us without mercy. Partner pulled his wadded-up handkerchief from his back pocket and removed his wrinkled straw hat. He glanced over at me as I stopped hoeing and leaned on my hoe, trying to catch my breath. As he swiped the rag across his forehead a couple of times, and wiped out the inside of his hat he wryly commented, "You know I wuz a mean baby before I wuz born…"

I gave him a quizzical look, thinking what in the world does he mean by that? I said, "Partner, what are you talkin' about, 'mean before you wuz born'? How can that be?" I guess I was expecting some cow pens theology, as Partner was prone to give on occasion.

He said, "Wellsir, it's this away…When I wuz bein' carried by my mama, before I wuz born, she was workin' in the garden settin' out little cabbage plants…"

"And…?" I asked, prompting him for the punch line.

With twinkling eyes, smiling sweetly, he said, "Well, I remember I kept reachin' out and pullin' 'em up…"

The mental image of that is still vivid to me to this day…

Years after we'd worked together, when Partner retired after some forty-years of service, in front of the gathered men at the shop, Paw told him to go down to Gilbert's Chevrolet in Okeechobee and pick out "any truck that suited him." Partner looked down at the ground, acting as if he was a little embarrassed. He shifted his weight a little, pushed his hat back on his head, and smiled, saying, "Y'all don't need ta do that…" But Paw told him how much he and Sonny appreciated his time there and how the whole crew appreciated him. Though reluctant, he later went to the dealership and selected a white Chevrolet truck. Even though he could have picked out any one they had, he chose a modest truck. It suited him.

Later, Partner returned for part-time work. The last time I saw him he was riding that old red lawn mower, pulling a small wagon full of dead cabbage palm fans. His old raggedy straw hat cocked back off his forehead. He was humped over the steering wheel, elbows resting on the wheel. As he pulled to a stop, shutting off the hot engine, he displayed a big grin as I approached him. We shook hands and grinned at each other. His hands were still coarse and rough. His fingernails were still long, in case, no doubt, he wanted to pick a dollar off a smooth surface. All the hard work times and joys of them flashed through my mind as I studied his old tired face. It was still sunburned low on his three-day beard and white as a lily on the upper portion. We visited a while, but not near enough…Ever have a heart ache when you think of friends of long ago? Boy, I miss him.

UNCLE DICK DURRANCE, a man that Partner talked a lot about, used to help some at the ranch as the brand man. Uncle Dick was from a pioneer family that settled in South Florida many years ago. Built like a bull walrus, he was slow as molasses. He wore a short-brimmed hat that was closer to a riverboat gambler derby than a cowboy hat. This only exaggerated his bulk. His branding iron was often a little too cold for a quick branding. "You brand like Dick Durrance" became a complaint when you didn't keep your branding iron hot. Also, "That's tighter'n Uncle Dick's hatband." I heard the phrase later at other places and marveled that everybody knew about "Dick's hatband". For some reason, they didn't use the "uncle" with it.

Uncle Dick was known also for his "opportunistic frugality." Mama thought it remarkable how he had an uncanny ability to time his visit just as we sat to supper and there was always an extra plate around somewhere. Seems to me that he was a Baptist preacher, too, preaching at the Ft Basinger Baptist Church. On occasion he'd try his evangelistic thrusts at Paw, or anyone else who'd listen, probably just practicing next week's sermon. They enjoyed each other's company. They'd ride in the Jeep some. Dick would have to work at getting in and out, grunting a bit from the efforts. I've seen them sit in the living room in front of the fire, not saying a word, for an hour or more. Paw might even look at a magazine while Uncle Dick quietly looked around at nothing in particular. He'd interlock his fingers on his belly and idly twiddle his thumbs. Abruptly Uncle Dick would get up, wheezing, "Frank, I got to go…" Paw would tell him, "Well, dodge the Yankees," a phrase we often used to indicate the prevalent driving habits of the winter tourists. Not much else was said. It was interesting to me to see two men so comfortable with their friendship that talking was unnecessary.

LUTHER CALHOUN came to the ranch after I arrived. He first struck me as being a bit of an outlaw. He told me that he had been in prison once or twice, never revealing the reason. He was usually unshaven at work and was as toothless as a rooster—except on weekends when he wore his teeth. I never knew if he shared them with anyone else during the week. Mama said he was handsome when he was clean-shaven, with his hair combed and dressed up with his store-bought teeth shining in his smile. Luther could do general ranch and grove work. He loved to drive tractors or any job where he could ride. He also could ride a horse and work in the cow pens though his Georgia brogans and thin saggy denim jeans were a tad out of place. I remember his saying to my mother at dinner one day with seven other cowboys bellied-up to the table, "You sure ain't gonna have trouble gettin' a cow crew here at this place with all these good groceries." Reeda once offered him ice cream when the other men had pecan pie. He was affronted at the oversight, asking for pecan pie as well. She was amazed that he could eat pecan pie without his teeth.

Luther really was a piece of work. I soon learned that he was crafty. He could slip into a place, gator hunt, fish or "borrow oranges," then slip out without leaving a hint of his passing. Luther looked out for Luther first. He admonished me to slow down on my tree hoeing, commenting, "You're makin' me look bad." He said you needed to stretch out the work so you wouldn't just have to go do something else. Luther was notorious about really working when the boss man came by. He'd slow back down soon, though, into a steady pace. He chewed Apple chewing tobacco, which often left yellow stains at the corners of his mouth. He was married to a much younger woman. She once remarked to me that she'd rather be an old man's nurse than a young man's slave. I think he was a renegade, somewhat like a retired pirate without the eye patch, hook and squawking green parrot. Hubert referred to him as, "That ol' gator." Luther spent a lot of time trying to impress the "boss man" with his skill and care. Of course, bringing fresh vegetables from his garden helped in that regard. I can still see him cleaning his coke-bottle thick glasses and getting another chew of Apple. We would still manage to get a lot of work done. I liked him a lot even with his idiosyncrasies. With that winning smile, he would have made a great politician…especially if it was his day to wear the false teeth.

JESSE POTTS, better known as Purty Jesse, was born near Paducah, Kentucky, and came in a roundabout way to Florida. He knew the area where I was born, but never spoke much about how he came to the ranch. I don't know when he came there. He was conscientious, dutifully working at any assigned task as if he were the only responsible one there. Jesse Potts was a religious man, too, showing his confident faith in God. Though he didn't preach like Partner or Uncle Dick, he was quick to join in on the mini-sermons that they delivered. He was experienced in manual labor, not having skills like heavy equipment operation, though he drove tractors well. His main tasks centered on the essential little things that made the homes, ranch and groves work efficiently. In the groves, Purty Jesse planted new re-sets trees, hoed, fertilized, and pruned in about every grove. He built fence, mowed lawns, landscaped and kept things clean and presentable. He usually didn't have to be told what to do; he knew and proceeded without a lot of instruction. Purty Jesse was a jack of all trades. He has continued to work on the ranch until he retired last year.

UGLY JESSE, whose last name I never knew, was much older than the other grove workers. A quiet man, he worked slowly but steadily, wore bib overalls and brogans and brought a sack lunch from a little café where he caught a ride to work. Most of the men brought a sack lunch – some grease-spotted from fried chicken, ham- or sausage-biscuits or some other fried meat. Whatever they brought, it was wrapped in wax paper that somehow didn't prevent soiling the brown paper sack. Ugly Jesse and Purty Jesse, as well as Partner, carefully stashed their lunches securely in the work truck, in a place inaccessible to dogs or meandering raccoons.

Once when we were building a fence in the marsh behind the house, Ugly Jesse had his left elbow over a post while stapling barbed wire to it. The wire broke and snapped away, cutting a 4-5 inch gash in his arm. It did a number on him and slowed him down some. I think someone took him to the shop for first aid, but he refused to go to the hospital. The next day, his arm was wrapped in a strip of a white sheet. He had some kind of wound dressing on it. It healed and left a nasty scar. We marveled at his toughness. Ugly Jesse was not a Cracker, but he was as tough as one. Nobody made much over the fact.

JAMES SHAW is the last of the original grove crew that I knew well. He is still at the ranch as I write. James was the meekest and gentlest man of the lot. He had a kind, friendly nature, quick to smile and laugh. He drove many of the machines, as well as did the grunt work, hoeing, hand-applying citrus fertilizer and every other thing he was asked to do. James even did a bit of pen work when we were cow hunting. I know a man, Dr. Charles Payton, who once said something that I stored in the back closet of my mind. In reference to an individual that was being considered for a prominent position, Charles said, "You know? I just can't think of anything bad to say about the man." In my recollection of James Shaw that same comment comes to mind.

SUSIE GLASS was another wonderful character. Not long after Queen, the first cook, quit, Suzie Glass returned to the ranch. She had worked there before as cook and housekeeper. Paw contacted her near Atlanta, Georgia, asking if she would come back to Florida. It didn't take long for her to settle into the little guesthouse about forty-five yards from the house. She talked funny, sort of like the quacking of a duck. She asked Paw to hold her money each week and only took a little for necessities like Sue Bee snuff, etc. So when vacation time came, she had two weeks coming and a considerable amount of money saved for her trip. He warned her once, "Suzie, don't you let anybody see that you have this money; they'll knock you in the head and take it away from you." She said, "Naw, Mr. Frank, I won' let nobody sees it." The next morning she appeared in her spotless, heavily starched white dress, ready for the ride to the bus station, She walked up to him, lifted her skirts and said, "Mr. Frank, cans ya sees mah finances?"

She had on white bloomers, her skinny little legs sticking out of the knee-length underwear. She had pinned her "finances" inside the bloomers. Repressing his startled chuckle, he answered, "No Suzie, I can't see your finances." We enjoyed Susie's phrase for years. Occasionally he'd ask Mama, "Cans ya sees my finances?"

These people made the backbone of the crew. Purty Jesse, Ugly Jesse, James and Luther showed me the ropes in the groves, though Luther was a fair hand in the pens. Hubert and Sonny taught me how they worked cattle and equipment. Suzie was faithfully there before daylight to fix me runny eggs, bacon and biscuits. She used spaghetti in her vegetable soup.

These are only introductions to people that I would learn to trust. They quickly accepted me, especially when I didn't back away from work. One once commented, "If'n I wuz you, I'd be settin' on my butt 'stead of doin' this grove work..." His comment reminded me of the story of the railroad president stepping out of his executive's coach to talk to a lineman. One of the officials asked him who was that man laying track and why was he talking to him. The president replied, "We started working for the railroad the same day. He worked for $1.50 an hour but I worked for the railroad." I wondered if this applied here. I guess I wasn't content to do manual labor all my life. But I was learning what it took to make the ranch work and it made it easy to fall into the scheme of things. But, boy, I had a lot to learn. In a way, it was like boot camp...

Reeda Williamson

My Mother was a Kentucky Cracker

"You grow up the day you have the first real laugh at yourself."
-Ethyl Barrymore

REEDA Frances Walden Jones Williamson was a Kentucky Cracker. I don't believe I would do introductions well if I did not include my mother. Each of the names was a division in her life. She was a Walden, had been married to my father, and finally married her soul mate.

I realize most everybody's mother is special. But my mother was different; she, like me, had no problem adapting to the Florida Cracker culture. However, she did add her own idiosyncrasies. For instance, she was a little standoffish with strangers, yet she could go up to a king and introduce herself. It generally took her a little time to get to know someone. Once you were a friend she could trust, she was yours for life. Loyalty was her strong suit but she had a tendency to remember wrongs done to her or her's a little too long…My stepfather helped her lighten up some, occasionally saying, "Let it go, Reeda…"

Some of my fondest memories are those related to their conversations. She had quite a bit of venom left in her from childhood and early life. When I'd come in from the woods and sit down with them, I'd hear some of the poison coming out and Paw would sit there and listen, without any condemnation.

Sometimes she'd tell him, "Frank, I need to talk." He'd put down his U.S. News and World Report, focus on her and reply, "Well, go ahead, Gal Baby." He'd light a cigar, look at her, and let her go on and on, saying nothing during the protracted venting. Obviously they didn't talk about personal things in front of me, but things that related to Mama, him and me were fair game. He'd just look at her, rolling and smoking that panatela cigar, with eyes twinkling. From time to time, he'd offer some consolation, some soothing and healing balm. This lack of any disapproval was just what she needed. She'd mellow ever so gradually, finally she'd settle down. She was like a confused teenager, only the last ten minutes of the conversation counted, the rest was just venting. It was as if she would test the limits of his patience, of his endurance. As her confidence in him was confirmed, her color would return, the lines would soften in her face. She'd become content again when she realized he understood. Each time she went through these episodes, she'd come out the better. She, too, was healing.

Reeda would go with him in the Jeep when they wanted to talk. That green Jeep was a place of contemplation for her as well. I imagine they talked a lot about these and other things, her sitting on the dip in the seat where the dogs' butts fit. He'd usually summarize what she was getting at: "So you're saying that they thought you did wrong? Well, who cares what they think. It doesn't amount to a hill of beans. Lighten up on yourself, Gal." Sometimes I know he didn't say much but she would come back content nonetheless. Maybe the key to his success with her was just listening. After a particularly difficult discussion, he'd say to me, "Boy, you better toss your hat in the house before you go in there. Reeda's been eatin' Kentucky ham today. She's plumb venomous." He'd kid her when she'd get on a tear. He'd pause, smiling at her with devilment and ask, "Have you been eatin' ham again?" She'd burst out laughing.

Her choices of phrases and sayings were "Crackerish". She had one expression that I found funny, one I've not heard anywhere else. If we were delayed in coming home at meal time for any reason, as we came in the door, she'd say, "Where have y'all been? I've been worried sick." I don't think she realized how out of context it was.

After I married and we had our first baby, we were living in Texas in the Air Force. We drove to Florida for Christmas one year and couldn't find a room for the night the whole way. Hunter, sick baby and I drove straight through. We pulled in the drive way at four o'clock in the morning, exhausted. She met us at the door with that familiar greeting, "Well…where have y'all been? I was worried sick…" Now the odd thing was she didn't expect us until the next day. (Paw opened the upstairs window and hollered, "Y'all are gonna have to pay for a full night.") Both greetings were music to us.

The use of this phrase so tickled me that it just naturally became implanted in my vocabulary. I'm amused at the expressions of people that I say it to when they come to the entrance of our church. I think that when we see her in heaven the first thing she'll say is, "Well where have y'all been…"

Mama didn't tolerate heat well. She'd use a phrase I still use today: "I got so hot that sweat just pooled in the dimple of my neck", referring to the junction of the clavicles and the base of the neck. Or, "The hair on the back of my head wuz ringing wet." I never understood why only the back of her head got wet with perspiration. And, to her, "ringing wet" meant that one could twist it to wring out the water like a wet towel. If she was hungry at noon, she'd say, "My Rice Krispies gave out about ten o'clock…"

All my childhood I heard a peculiar descriptive phrase from her. When she came into the room early in the morning, especially before daylight, she might not be in the usual pristine beauty that she obtained after applying the paints and plasters that women use for make-up. We never noticed if she was not all primped up. Maybe she was just very sleepy and hadn't combed her hair well, usually because she was running a little late in preparing a meal. She'd say, "I know I must look like a wild woman from Borneo." As a little tike I had wild imaginations of what a wild woman from Borneo looked like. It wasn't until National Geographic published the pictures that I fully understood.

My mother had a peculiar way of calling us to the table. One of the things that galled her was being tardy for dinner, as if the food would immediately lose all flavors or become poison if you didn't eat it immediately. She believed that everyone should instantly move to the table on the first call, which we usually did. If there was a particularly important situation which distracted us, such as the last play of the Orange Bowl, she'd impatiently call out, "Y'all come on or I'll throw it to the hogs…" We didn't have any hogs. Here again, this came from deep in her rural Kentucky childhood pool of expressions.

When reaching for a second helping, she rationalized, "I think I'll have another piece of pie to get this taste out of my mouth…" It was common for her to ask a question to no one in particular at the dinner table. The table would be full of half empty serving dishes: Meat, three vegetables, a green salad, a fruit salad, a starch, pickles or olives, fresh bread or rolls, three kinds of drinks and one or two desserts. Then it would come, "Well, what do y'all want for supper?" Most everyone was stuffed at this point. The last thing we wanted to think about was more food. I would groan, "Leftovers…" This satisfied her but she looked as if it were a novel idea, silently asking, "Are you sure?" She never believed us, that her leftovers were fit for royalty.

Usually she'd return from a church dinner or family reunion where "dinner on the ground" was the order of the day with, "Why, there was enough food for a wheat thrashin'." She'd never attended a meal for wheat thrashers.

Where did that come from? Or a large amount of a particular food was "a foot tub full." Being somewhat expert in authentic bar-be-cue, she had little tolerance for an inferior, non-Kentucky type. She was disgusted with tomato paste sauces or ones that were plain sorry. She'd say things like, "Their bar-be-que wadn't fit to eat. They had tomato catsup gobbed all over it…" Her status as expert in this area had credibility since she'd made considerable effort to eat bar-be-que (and country ham) at every place south of the Mason-Dixon Line. We knew what she meant by "gobbed". Synonyms for gobbed were slathered, piled, covered, hidden, concealed, doctored, or in some way treated to try to improve an otherwise inferior product. I never ate bar-be-que anywhere that she had labeled substandard.

After a meal, when there was a lull in conversation, she'd sometimes slowly and deliberately wave her hand over the table. It was obvious what she was doing, but, you know, those dishes never did disappear. She would smile like it might have worked or that she was just not good it.

They enjoyed summers at their North Carolina mountain cabin where she canned all kind of fresh produce from the garden. She had an area dedicated to freezing and canning in the basement. On one occasion, they returned to discover that her canning room had been looted of her whole summer's work. Every jar of jam, preserves and vegetables was gone. A car with a South Carolina license tag had been going down the hill as they had turned into the driveway. From that day forward she referred to anyone with a South Carolina tag who committed even the slightest infringement of the rules of the road as, "Look at that South Carolina trash…", reminding us that she'd been wronged by some thieves from that fine state at one time. She took that as the ultimate violation of one's being. Stealin' one's home-canned goods was as low as you could get, certainly deserving imprisonment, or worse.

She'd also brought up some phrases from Kentucky that confused listeners a bit. They'd catch up with her by the context. For instance, if something was broken, unfixable or just plain frustrating, she'd say, "We ought to throw that thing *down the hill*." That made no sense until one realized that she was reared in the rolling hills of Western Kentucky where trash was thrown down a hill way back behind the home place. Occasionally, there'd be a mass burial of sorts where the old broken bottles, plates, pans, furniture, or fire place ashes and anything else would be covered. Until that burial all of the children loved the "down-the-hill" site since there were all kinds of treasures there. She did start changing the phrase to, "We ought to haul that thing to the garbage pile", referring to where we burned trash way back behind the house. Another phrase, "Well...that cut his water off..." came from one of her first jobs at the Henderson City Water Department. She was the receptionist and handled all water service complaints. When she'd get exasperated at a customer for repeated non-payment of water bills and a multitude of lame excuses, she'd tell one of the employees to go cut their water off, which of course, brought a new round of complaints of her being unfair, though she wasn't. But the phrase meant to her that she'd reached her limit in patience, that the cuttee was out of business and they now had a critical problem from their self-inflicted irresponsibility. In her mind, "Boy... that just cut his water off..." meant he had fouled his nest in some way and was now suffering the consequences.

But one of the most predictably funny things was her way of saying "I told you so..." If some ill-conceived plan didn't work out she'd say, "I tried to tell you..." or "If you'da asked me I coulda told you..." What made it funny was that she may have said nothing to you regarding the activity or not known about it in the first place. The idle comment sometimes was followed by, "Maybe next time you'll know..." (Know what? That she would second-guess you again?) And, as the phrase was common in her family in Kentucky, she'd sometimes expand it to, "I tried to tell you...(Long pause) but naw, you wouldn't listen to me..." It was so funny to me that when she'd say the first part, I'd finish with, "But naw...I wooden listen to you..." She'd grin when she realized she'd said it.

And my friends wonder why I have an overdeveloped "gift" of embellishment...

I remember Mama's cooking for the cowboys during cow hunting. She had Queen as helper and housekeeper, but Queen didn't always do things to suit her. There'd be about eight hearty men show up for breakfast, dinner and supper. She'd start early. By 5:30 am, she'd have pies made and breakfast going when Queen got there. Queen was a piece of work. She had worked for years at a headskin called "The Twin Oaks Cafe" in Okeechobee. When someone asked her why she quit the café, she indignantly responded, "Well, I wuz workin' from 6 'til 6 and they changed my hours to 8 'til 8—I wuz not gonna work a extra two hours and not git paid for it."

She was a little too laid back for my mother's way of doing things. She quit and Mama stayed on.

The cowboys ate all the groceries she prepared and loved them. Luther Calhoun told her, "Miz Williston, we ain't never worked anywheres that fed pecan pie before." (Luther never did get her name right. It was "Mr. Frank and Miz Williston"; Sonny and I used it when we imitated Luther.)

Mama started early making the noon meal. Once the breakfast dishes were done, she'd have dinner going by 9:00. We'd pile in at noon, eat, rest under the shade trees out front for about 30 minutes, then load up and go back to work.

It was hard to get going again after her ample meals. A "fat nap" under a shade tree really helped. You had to watch out when taking a nap, however. You could wake up with your feet tied together with rawhide strips or patties of dried cow manure on your chest or spider or tree frog in your hat. Anything was fair game. They all relished this sport.

At dark, suppers would be leftovers and additional dishes: beans and rice, chicken-fried steak or roast beef, gravy, green beans, potatoes, various salads, scratch biscuits and macaroni and cheese. She'd make banana pie, chess pie, apple pie, pecan or chocolate pie, Mississippi Mud and pineapple up-side-down cakes. I think she loved watching people eat her cooking. Some people say that's the mark of a good cook.

At one quiet supper, after the flurry of cowboys had gone home, Paw told her of a time when the cowboys were fed out in the woods and a camp cook prepared food for all the crew. They ate beans, potatoes, rice, tomato gravy (made like cream gravy, but with a can of tomatoes), swamp cabbage stew and fried meat. He said that they complained one day about eating the same ol' thing. He told the cook to take orders for what the men wanted. Canned peaches were top of the list. So the cook went to town and bought two cases of canned peaches. Paw said he thought they would bankrupt him. They ate the new menu but after a few days, were back asking for beans, rice, tomato gravy, swamp cabbage and meat. Apparently there just aren't enough calories in peaches to keep men working cattle.

Reeda had another notable trait that impressed me. She had this thing for diamonds. In her mind, one had arrived if one had a big diamond, and she had a two caret ring. Now the funny thing to us was that she rarely wore it. She had a three-caret zirconium imitation, set in the identical mounting. The real one was in the safety deposit box at the bank. She stated her logic as: "Well, as long as you own a real one it doesn't matter if you wear a fake…" Otherwise, she was painfully frugal. We fondly remember the incongruity when she would get into her Cadillac with her $ 150, three-caret zirconium ring shining in the sun, and made her way to Wal Mart to buy a $6 cotton blouse and shower shoes on sale and then driving across town to save 2 cents per gallon on gas. "You can take the gal out of Kentucky, but you can't take the Kentucky out of the gal…" But a more tender-hearted and loyal person could not be easily found. The last thing she did on earth, the morning she died, was to write two checks. One was to pay her phone bill, the other a generous donation to the Billy Graham Evangelistic Association.

When my Mama died, a whole tradition of Kentucky farm cooking died with her. When asked why didn't she learn to make chicken and dumplings, my step-sister Biba said she didn't need to know how because, "Reeda was so good at it, why bother?" (To me this is a play on the old "If you own a dog, you don't have to bark" principle.)

Introduction to Cow Huntin'
with Florida Crackers

"Cracker: a person or device that cracks; a thin crisp wafer of un-leavened dough, sometimes called a biscuit; an impoverished white person in the rural South, especially in Georgia and Florida, as a contemptuous term; or, a generations-old term for Florida cowboy or cow hunter, derived from the 'cracking' sound of their cowhide whips, an instrument whose crack could startle and discipline a herd (or an individual bull, cow or dog) and be heard for miles. To-day, the term is still in wide use in Florida. It is not to be taken as pejorative. In reality, it is usually associated with Florida cowboys."
-HSJ

LEAVING all that was familiar, plunging into a new culture, there were questions. How could a boy from Western Kentucky feel so immediately at home in the midst of them? How could I be so comfortable in this new do-main? It was a natural fit for me. I had little trouble in communication and understanding. I had their general common-sense attitude and an apprecia-tion of their keen humor. Ever since my first days at the ranch I've thought the term "Cracker" had a broader meaning. It didn't take long to become sure of it; there was more than meets the eye when it came to these people. Their good-natured humor made the transition much easier.

I fell right naturally into a routine of traveling the ranch, but one day I was alerted by the talk at the machine shop about an up and coming activ-ity. Dentureless Luther sidled up beside me, spit a gob of "Apple" Chewing Tobacco toward a dozing chameleon and drawled, "Hiard, you gonna help us out when we cow hunt?" That intrigued me (not the spitting, I had seen that before, the question.). What in the world was he talking about? Cow hunt? There was a palpable eagerness in the air. June was the month for working cattle, of "cow huntin'", as the Crackers called it. It was like a spring round up, only they did it in the heat of the Florida June. On one of our ambling trips through the marshes and hammocks, Paw and I discussed my helping work the cows and calves. Judging from the gleam in his eyes I gathered that I would be a fool not to participate. He said, "Biba, Charles, David and Susan are coming. Charles takes a month's leave from the Air Force to help. You might as well git in the middle of it..." I hadn't been there very long and didn't know exactly what would happen, but it sure sounded like fun to me.

I heard the term came from Crackers of the olden days when there were no fences—they went out into the woods, actually hunting the cattle. The cowboys would spend considerable amounts of time studying the habits and patterns and hiding places of the cattle before any attempt was made to gather them, sometimes for weeks. The older Cracker cowboys were canny about tracking cattle, knowing their habits and tendencies. They'd have the cattle located before first light, on the edge of a big marsh or in the hammocks. If the mosquitoes were bad the cattle would come out of the marshes, heading for the higher ground of the piney flatwoods, the scrubs or hammocks. The good news was that most of the herd would bunch up when they saw you. But there were the few who'd go their own way, striking out for parts known only to them. It was just like handling people—ten percent of your customers usually gave you ninety percent of your problems.

The first time I heard the cow whips cracking in the woods, the term "Cracker" made sense to me. It sounded like a .22 caliber rifle fired off in the woods, followed by a yip or high falsetto whoop. The whips were of braided leather used to drive cattle out of the thick woods. Many think that is the reason Florida cowboys are called Crackers, but I now think there is a little more to it than that. You could hear them a long ways off. They would wind up their whips overhead with a soft "ch-wohup" (like a fishing rod swooshed through the air), a slight pause, then a resounding "POW".

There are "Georgia Crackers," too. I am not sure how they got their name. I expect it was pejorative, originally meaning poor white rural Southerners. It could have come from their use of whips to work with mules. Nevertheless, a good man with his whip could just about knock a fly off a cow's ear without disturbing the animal. It is a skill that has largely been lost in modern times. Whips were part of the Cracker cowboy's gear. You still see them used at commercial Florida ranches, but many are now hanging on walls next to mounted deer horns, like trophies in a museum. You could lightly snap a cow on the rump as she was stalling at a gate or strike a bad bull on the nose as he bowed up in the pens – to encourage them to move along. It was an excellent means of getting their attention and a pop would get a mean dog's attention, too. You'd have to be careful to avoid the backlash. Your face would smart for hours. I learned this lesson several times.

I reckon you never really get to know people until you work closely with them. Having a common goal or trial helps sort out and emphasize the character of men. I had a lot to learn about people, especially about these cowboys. They were ordinary men doing extraordinary things. How does one sum up the character of a man? It would take time to fully appreciate their unique personalities. I entered the world of some remarkable individuals.

Alrite, You Got your Hat, Gloves and Boots but You Cain't Work Cattle without a Horse

"I have come home at last! This is my real country! I belong here. This is the land I have been looking for all my life, though I never knew it till now…"
-C. S. Lewis' Unicorn, from *The Voyage of the Dawn Treader*

NOW about this cow huntin' business, I had no good idea what I was in for. My first thought was, "Who me…ride a horse?" I was to meet everyone at the horse barn at or before daylight. I got up, showered, ate the big breakfast Mama prepared and walked down to the machine shop, catching a ride with the first man who came by. By the time we got to the barn, Hubert had things moving along. He lived in the house near the barn so it wasn't anything to him to get there early. Besides, he'd been up two hours or more, as he'd say, "Drinkin' coffee and smokin' cigarettes." Under dim barn lights, he'd opened stall doors, put a big measure of horse feed in the feed pans, and call a loud "Whoop…Come on…" out into the dark horse pasture. You'd hear them coming like a herd of buffalo. Into the alleyway of the barn they'd run, stirring up dew dampened dust, sorting themselves into open stalls, backing ears, squealing and fussing at competitors. After a few days of this ritual, most got the idea and would be waiting nearby. Sometimes, one horse was cantankerous about coming in, but would relent when he heard the crunching of grain by the others.

These horses were not your let's-go-for-a-Sunday-afternoon-ride type. They were strictly-business working horses. A few of them would snort and flare their nostrils, rolling their eyes and giving the distinct impression that a blow-up could occur. I found that the best approach was to move in slow deliberate movements, speaking softly, giving the horse time to size you up. Saddles were kept on saw-horses attached to the walls; the bridles hung on nails nearby. The tack room smelled of dust, horse feed, saddle oil and leather, and of age. In these early mornings the room was unoccupied. Later in the day, most times, when you went to get your saddle, there was a chicken or two in there, making a livin' salvaging spilled grain. They'd panic as you darkened the doorway.

True Cracker horses were a little smaller and thinner than the rodeo types, but they were hardened, tough, stubborn and more often than not reliable. Usually about 900 to 950 pounds, not always well broke, they could kick the taste out of your mouth if you weren't careful. They reminded me of the mustang. Also I wondered if there wasn't some of the old Spanish horse blood in their veins from ones abandoned when the original explorers left Florida. Perhaps these horses were adopted by the first cow hunters, the Seminoles. There are still many around the ranches of Florida. Capable of working in extreme conditions, they have proved themselves to be just right for the Florida environment. Today, roping and rodeo horses, racers and runners, and special-use horses have infused Quarter horse genetics and that of other breeds into Cracker horse bloodlines. The modern one looks more like a Quarter Horse than the old small, tough woods horses of years ago.

Many ranches had typical bays, browns, blacks, speckled and blazed-faced cow horses. A few had heavy muscled Quarter horse types, but I suspect they didn't have the stamina and heat tolerance. By analogy, the Cracker horse was a shotgun, the Quarter horse a rifle. Cracker horses were around but there was mostly a generic type of mixed bloodlines, moderately or thinly muscled, lean-tough, sturdy and strong, weighing about 1000 pounds.

Most of the ranch horses were named for some outstanding characteristic. I was assigned "Ol' Thunder and Lightning," shortened to "Thunder", a tall, buttermilk gelding. It didn't take me long to discover he lived up to his name. He'd jar your whole body like a close-by thunder and lightning strike. The choppiness of his gait and halts was caused by his straight fetlocks, the ankle and bones immediately above the hoof. There was no spring or cushioning in his fetlocks. He also had a terrible habit of fighting the bit when headed to the barn. He would clamp his front jaw teeth on it, pulling, tossing and jerking his big head this way and that. This was a constant aggravation for a tired rider. You had to be constantly holding him back or he'd run to the barn if you let him have his head. After a hard day in the saddle, from the far end of the ranch, he'd begin this headstrong backbone-jarring prance. I never broke him of it. I tried running him all day long to tire him out. It didn't work. It just made the trip back worse for me. The best I could do was to get him in a fast walk and hold him there, kinda like running wide open in first gear in the Jeep. Hubert cussed him, but he was able to smooth him out to a very fast walk where the bit's chin chain jingled in a steady rhythm. I never totally mastered the technique.

If I had named him, it would have been something like "Jackhammer.". We could have named him "Chiropractor" for the adjustments he made in our spines. I hated that horse for a long time, but he rarely stumbled or fell with me. I figured Sonny disliked him, too, for the pain he caused. Hubert just grumbled about him, calling him a jarhead or other colorful words he'd learned in the Navy. I don't think Hubert associated the name with the Marines. It was just a name he used. He descriptively used "jughead" as a nickname, too. But, in retrospect, they probably knew Thunder was sure-footed. Because of that one characteristic, he was probably the best horse for me; besides, I was the new kid on the block and didn't know any better.

Once while riding Thunder, a cow got away from the group. Trying to head her back to the herd, I sailed him into a bog at a full gallop. He never missed a beat, though he struggled a bit. Hubert caught up with me, warning me, "Stepandfetchit, you can git hurt bad doin' that…If he bogs down and throws you off, you could break your neck…" It never happened again.

There was a sorrel mare there at that time, appropriately named "Red", more typical of a Thoroughbred than a Quarter Horse. They didn't let me get anywhere near her until later in my training. She was undoubtedly the fastest mare I ever rode. Sonny won many a bet racing her. He warned me to never give her head; I did, Once. Like to have scared me to death! The acceleration was unbelievable. She was wide open in about three lunges. When I finally did get her under control, there were wide grins all around, knowing looks back and forth among the crew. The unspoken message: "I bet he don't try that agin." Mama's advice would have applied here: "I tried to tell you…"

They warned me about not running a horse through a pine thicket, saying that he could cut close to the trees and duck under limbs leaving little room for your knees, head and body. Again, I tried it anyway. Once. They were right, again. After a few days the pain subsided in my knees, ankle and shoulder. I was young then, wiry and tough. Pain was something you didn't dwell on much. This pain tolerance served me well years later.

I named another gelding "Toothbrush" because he had the habit of rinsing out his mouth at the water trough – the name stuck. Another example was "Sailboat", a filly, because it was like changing tack on a sailing yacht when you tried to turn her. You'd pull her head to turn her in one direction or the other and she'd sail out way past the point you'd plan to turn, making a wide America's Cup curve. This activity was particularly invigorating at high speed, when she tended to run away. When she did take a notion to run away, pulling her head around into your lap would usually get her under control.

Everybody's favorite mare was "Ol' Dixie." She was a stocky Palomino Quarter horse with the characteristic flaxen mane and tail. Paw picked her out during a horse buying trip. He dickered with the seller about some colts he really didn't want, while surreptitiously eyeing this exceptional filly from a distance. Her temperament, as well as her muscle and joint conformation were excellent.

On and on they dickered over the prices and the pros and cons of the decoy colts: too straight in the legs, poor foot conformation, pig-eyed, too skinny or just crazy. Finally, when he thought he had the seller worn down, Paw asked him what he would take for the Palomino filly. The man mentioned a figure that was much lower than her actual worth. It was not well thought out; he assumed that Mr. Frank was just making conversation. But to his surprise, "Sold!" was the answer. A deal's a deal, the filly was his.

Dixie was the most wonderful mare one would ever hope to ride. It was like getting into a luxury limousine after riding in a coal truck. She moved at the slightest touch of the reins. She was easy on the butt and thighs and when she loped it was like sitting in a rocking chair on the front porch. Dixie only had one idiosyncrasy: she occasionally decided that she didn't want to be tied by her reins and would, with all her considerable strength, pull back until they broke. One moment she'd be standing there, three-legged relaxed and the next, "Hey, I think I'll break the reins today…" Her haunches would drop down, front legs stiffen, head thrust high in the air, and wild-eyed, she'd just start to back up. The leather reins would creak as they stretched, then "POW" they'd go, no rhyme or reason. She'd calmly mosey off to a gate or into an open stall, looking around as if saying, "Did y'all see that?" You could easily catch her, hold her by the mane or halter and start the repairs or replacement. It would be twenty years before I would learn how to stop this behavior, but then we just chalked it up to "that's just Ol' Dixie". Sonny, Partner, Charles and a few others rode her, especially the beginners and novices. But I only rode her a few times, because by the time I met her, she was a little aged. By then, Partner had dibs on her.

Once saddled and mounted, off we went through the horse pasture to work. The horses instinctively liked to stay together, snorting noisily on these early trips, like old men clearing their throats and noses the first thing in the mornings. The sound carried a long ways in the cool, damp woods. Saddle leather squeaked. Men talked about humorous or personal things before the day's plan and instructions were given.

Usually Sonny or Hubert knew where the cattle were likely to be at that early time of day. Hubert would warn us of potential difficulties and where to be especially careful in cleaning an area of cattle. Assignments were given; groups of two or three were told to be at a location at an approximate time: "Don't show yerselves 'till you see or hear us come out of the hammock. Be sure that the double gates are closed. Don't crowd 'em at the bridge. Try to keep 'em away from that old fence at the Raulerson Grove. Y'all take the dogs with you; that's the only way you can clean out that hammock. If one of you shows hisself at the edge of the marsh, they'll start driftin' toward the hammock." Commands were in the if-y'all-want-to suggestion form. There was considerable time spent in discussing what to do if things didn't go according to plan. Most of the discussions were done on the way; sometimes while sitting on horseback at a gate where we were to split up. One or two would turn off at some point, circling around to cut off escape routes. The first several trips I was totally dependent on following someone. I had no idea how things were inter-related nor did I have any cow sense. As the weeks progressed and I paid attention, I began to catch on.

It was quite a time for a young fella. Now and then someone would have an altercation with his frisky ride on these mornings, especially if it was chilly. But these "you-horse, me-rider" squabbles were quickly settled. Wet myrtle bush limbs lightly slapped your legs as your horse passed them. The early morning sounds were unique to this area: the rustle of spring-back palm fronds, the crackle and pop of dry palm boots and limbs under the horses' feet. Big spider webs delicately hooked limbs together – you had to hold an arm in front of you to avoid a face full of wet web or an ambitious spider. The moist air smelled fresh.

What was at first radically new and strange to me soon became routine. Cow huntin' days started at the horse barn. From that point on there was some variation in where we went and where and what we worked. I settled in. It felt like I had come home from an alien planet. Excitement, anticipation, and contentment filled my healing soul. Little did I imagine that in the future it would be my good fortune to observe, eat, hunt and share humorous stories over camp coffee while working in many different cow pens from Sarasota to Ft Pierce, from Gainesville to Clewiston. Nor could I have ever anticipated the development of my love for Florida history.

Introduction to Brahman Cattle

What we most love and revere generally is determined by early associations.
-Oliver Wendell Holmes, Jr.

ON the early Jeep ride-abouts I had already noticed a breed very much unlike the common squatty fat Kentucky cattle. Enormous animals, they had big sagging ears, humps over the shoulders, pendulous loose skin under their necks, long legs and bodies and all kinds of colors from shaded grays to reds, tans, blacks, browns and speckled combinations. All were unfamiliar to me. The Brahman was one of the most intriguing creatures I saw in this new world. They just fit in the marshes, tall grasses, bay heads and boggy swamp-like parts of the unique Florida country. Most think of Florida as white beaches and motels, coconut palms and little drinks with umbrellas in them. Yes, I thought of Florida as mostly Miami-ish, too. But the land I now roamed was not at all like that. Here were rugged cattle in a natural and harsh environment. This was my introduction to Brahman cattle and it was to become very up-close and personal.

We called them "brahmas", pronounced by the Crackers as, "brammers". The crossbreeding program involved the use of Purebred Brahman bulls with cows of a variety of diverse genetic backgrounds. Some of the cows looked a little like the olden scrub cattle, descendents of cattle abandoned or lost by the Spanish. The Seminoles also were cattle herders, taking the Spanish cattle as they found them. Paw said at the time of the purchase of the ranch property there were some wild Spanish-type cattle roaming the woods and marshes. They were included with the property. Small, tough and mean Scrub Bulls were the sires of many calves, and served as the means of population for many generations. They didn't amount to anything like modern cattle. I heard old timers say that big scrub cattle weighed 600 to

700 pounds. Men could hand-catch and hold them for branding and ear-marking. But, Sir, you don't do that with an eleven-hundred pound cow or a three-quarter ton bull today. The ranch had other breeds of herd-sires, too. There were some half-crazy-long-as-a-train Charolais, huge beige-colored bulls whose origin was France. There were several "puzzle-gutted Angus bulls", as Sonny called them. I don't think he particularly liked the short-legged, stumpy conformation. They probably would do better on supple-mental feed. They did however sire some nice uniform black calves. Seems to me there were also some Polled Hereford bulls, in addition to the horned ones. Here again they weren't the tough kind that one sees today. This was a time when breeds were rapidly changing to more rugged, longer-legged frames, ones able to walk farther and better handle the heat of the South-eastern US. There was a steady change to bulls that would forage better and sire thicker and more standardized calves. The industry began to under-stand the inherent fertility of some breed lines and this was highly prized in selecting herd sires. There are Angus and Herefords today that would dwarf the ones of the sixties. Progressive animal scientists and producers began to develop Brahman and the English breeding programs where they "created or designed" whole new genetically stable breeds, such as Brangus, Braford, Santa Gertrudis and others. We also kept a herd of Purebred Brahman for producing our own Brahman bulls.

By the time I got to South Florida, there had been several generations of inter-breeding the Brahma bulls with the native cows, and there was still benefit to utilizing Brahma blood. It was a genetic phenomenon called hy-brid vigor, where the offspring of two genetically unrelated individuals re-sult in a calf that has better traits than either of the parents. The name of the game was pounds of beef at weaning time, a high number of cows conceiv-ing and having live calves and, also, in the case of our program at the time, increased heat tolerance and insect resistance of the crossbred cattle. The Brahma crossbreds were a superior animal on grass when compared to heat stressed English breeds such as Angus and Herefords. Other breeds required more feed while the Brahma crossbreds were better able to handle poorer quality grasses, as well as stress. Most of the cattlemen at the time didn't supplement their cattle. Many of the ranchers already owned their land or had so much pasture that they could leave the cattle alone.

Brahma cattle had most of these desired qualities, but were generally a lot ranker to handle. Armed with sharp horns, they were a terror for the man who was not concentrating. You didn't want to get caught asleep at the wheel, so to speak. The first lesson I learned about them was, "pay attention." Partner dryly commented about a cow that nearly caught him as he walked across the pens, "Why, she like to have scared my mule…"

Paw told me that Brahmas will not be driven, but can be led. He added that they were different from other breeds in handling characteristics, and to watch them closely to learn their behavior. The cow trails on the ranch were made from the Brahma crossbreds traveling in a line, behind a leader. This trait is still seen in India, the origin of the breed and everywhere Brahman are reared. He said things like, "Look ahead at the herd when movin' them. Anticipate what they're thinkin'. Don't let them take it away from you, if you can. Open gates and let them "discover it," making them think it was their idea. Sometimes if you'll jus' be quiet and sit your horse, they'll move themselves in the right direction." He indicated that how a ranch built or oriented their cow pens could make a difference in how well or poorly the cattle would handle. For example, if the cattle went down a chute in the general direction of their home pasture, they'd work better than those prodded in the other direction. They had an uncanny ability to know how to get back to their home pasture. We found this knowledge to be helpful after an unavoidable escape from the pens. We knew where to find them. More than once when a bull or cow jumped out of the pens or over a fence, I heard Hubert or Sonny say, "Let 'em go, we'll pick them up at the gate or the hammock."

The crossbred cows would "eat your sack lunch," as the men used to say, a euphemism for "hunt you up and try to gore you or your horse in the pens." They were not exactly like the wild steers of the pioneer West, who, like African Water Buffalo, would lie in thickets and ambush you. They were more likely to only give you a problem when they were cornered, had a calf to protect, or had no way to escape. The ones that were temporarily separated from the herd could be frantic and aggressive, especially if it was a mama cow with a baby. Bulls, too, didn't like to be isolated. "Turn in some ladies…he'll settle down", someone would say. Sure enough, putting cows in with a mean bull would smooth things out.

The first few weeks of my first cow huntin' happened to be during a particularly wet year. June was normally the rainy season. I remember drinking fresh-squeezed orange juice at daylight in the kitchen while looking out to the east toward Ft. Pierce, about thirty-five miles away. I saw cloud tops where big thunderheads were developing. It was usually expected that it would rain by 2:00 pm. I thought it peculiar that the rains were so predictable. The daily rains were so heavy that first summer that only about 6 inches of the fence posts in the pasture behind the house showed above the water. We rode the airboat out over pasture fences, skimming along at breath-taking speeds. The cattle headed for higher ground while the water slowly found its way to the drainage canals on the way to Lake Okeechobee. When the water levels returned to normal, submerged grass was exposed to the sun and had an unpleasant stale/sour smell as it dried in the heat.

When the sun returned after downpours, the cow pen was a humid hell-on-earth, but we managed. We didn't know any better than to keep working, nor did we much care. The winters were the dry months; the summers there were typically wet. Weather patterns came in cycles. Drought and flood years would come. The old Crackers warned that hurricanes would come in cycles, too. That year, our boots stayed wet most of the day. I spent a considerable amount of time drying out my soggy boots on the weekends, then waterproofing them on Sunday night.

In those days it was common to trade help with the other ranches. I met some notable Cracker characters that summer, like Junior Mills, Jack Page, Clifford Bennett and the Norman brothers. Sure enough, the first time I met them, the Norman crew from Dark Hammock Ranch showed up before daylight and after only cursory Monday morning greetings unloaded their saddled horses. Everyone still had the proverbial sleep in his eyes. Ephraim, Alfred and George Norman, were the backbone of their crew. Ephraim brought his son-in-law occasionally. I don't remember if they brought anyone else with them that first time.

The Normans, a pioneer family, grew up a little ways northwest of the ranch. I got to know them well when we traded help. Of all the Norman sons, Ephraim was one I best recall. He was short, lean, and feisty, having a bit of a cocky air about him, which wasn't irritating at all. It was probably just an expression of his confidence around cattle. Sonny called him the Bantam Rooster on occasion. I guess partly because he rode a stallion named Peanut instead of a mare or gelding. The first time he unloaded Peanut at the barn there was no doubt in my mind that he was one tough horse. Ephraim managed to control his aggressive stallion nature. There wasn't much Ephraim couldn't do on Peanut.

Alfred Norman was gregarious, slim, wiry and tougher than dry leather. And George, who I think was the oldest son, was a little heavier than the others. He was generally quieter, kind of like an owl among peacocks. I later knew their sister, Stella. She married a fine man named Charlie Rowland. Eventually the Norman estate was divided among all the kids when their daddy died. (Interestingly, over twenty years later I worked or rather "was worked" at the sister's ranch at Panther Ford, and Kent and Kurt Wall, two of the great-grandsons of Mr. Norman, worked for me at my veterinary clinic in Highlands County.)

We'd work our way across the ranch to the pastures, cutting across fields and roads. Once we located the cattle, they tended to gather together. We'd coax them into a tight bunch and one of us would ride ahead to give them someone to follow. A white horse worked best. I suppose it was the easiest for them to see. Of course, calves, yearlings, bulls and the outlaws weren't about to follow anyone. Instead, they'd dart toward any potential escape route. The cow dogs were indispensable here, efficiently keeping them gathered in a manageable group. Those determined cattle that decided to go it alone were met or circled and escorted back to the group, sometimes with a nipped nose or heel. These unique "assistants" relished their work with undisguised glee.

When bringing the cattle to the pens we slowed the pace. I fell in behind to plug open spaces in the line and here and there someone would crack a whip, especially in thick brush. On cool mornings the echo of a cracking whip could be heard a long way off. You could keep up with a man's location by the noise of his whips and his whoops and hollers to encourage the stragglers to move up. One of the men on occasion would break off a dry limb or cabbage palm fan as he rode under the tree. He'd pull a pocket knife and trim it down. This stick could be used to poke a straggler to join with the group or they'd "whoop" and slap bushes, brush or dried cabbage limbs with a sharp pop. I noticed that when you rode directly behind a cow, you could turn her to one side or the other. To guide one left, you rode to their right, behind or beside them. Cattle have a blind spot directly behind them, similar to one in a truck driver's mirror. One of the men told us that he was so little when he started cow huntin' that he couldn't yell very loudly. According to him he said, "I musta sounded like a piglet squealing", so his daddy made him carry a cow bell. He'd rattle it as he rode in the hammocks. I figured it served as a way to keep up with the boy as much as to drive the cattle.

Once we reached the pens, loaded a portion of the group into a holding pen, and started working the cattle, it was Knuckleville and Skint Finger City. We usually worked the adult cattle first, saving the calves until late in the afternoon. Many times we wouldn't finish till after dark. Nobody outwardly hoped for a rainstorm, but a rain was appreciated when it came. There were times when the rain breaks seemed few and far between (because you were looking for them) but they came almost daily that June. These holdups irritated Hubert. He'd pace under the open shed where we huddled. He'd fret a little, an occasional soft sigh coming from him as he watched the cattle. I think he was worried about lightning striking the fences where they bunched up, in addition to the loss of time. The cattle would hunker, turning their rumps into the direction of the wind, away from the sheets of rain, dropping their heads low and letting the water drip off their ears.

When I recall these times, not to stray too far from the subject, I remember vividly how common and close the lightning strikes were during those afternoon thunderstorms. Lightning was a real danger for the men and livestock. Standing under a tin roof by a metal chute in the pens was a fearful thing, but worse than that was being caught out in the open on horseback. Tall pines were attractors for these strikes. We were told not to go under trees when the lightning was bad. I recall it's hitting a dead pine right in front of the truck once. It made a sharp snap, instantly followed by a deafening clap of thunder. Ranchers sometimes found lightning-struck cows, with legs and hooves split where they had led the voltage to ground. I learned to immediately roll stunned cows onto their sternums or chests so they could relieve the swelling of the rapidly collecting rumen gas. The ruminant relies on a "fermentation vat" in their fore stomach. There, grasses are broken down to useful products for digestion. This gas production is ongoing and dynamic; they must belch up the gas, otherwise they would shortly become so swollen in the abdomen ("bloated") that asphyxiation would result. I heard of a man who witnessed three cows being struck by lightning next to a fence. He quickly went to them, and seeing they were dead, immediately starting butchering them for his freezer. People don't realize that lightning can hit as far as miles away from the generating cloud. (Ask Lee Trevino about his bout with lightning during a golf tournament. He said he always carried a One Iron in the fairways after being struck, adding that he didn't think even God could hit a One Iron…)

Paw told of the times he'd seen herds moving as thunderheads built; and that shimmering around the horns of the cattle there would be a blue cast. The cattle were agitated and jumpy, stampeding easily. "If you see that blue haze, get off your horse, and I mean now!" I heard others tell similar tales and warnings about this inland St. Elmo's fire. Several years later, on the Kissimmee River, I became a believer as our fishing rods hummed like miniature power lines. It didn't take me long to agree to pull in and head for home.

Wes, Sonny's son, told me he bought ten head from Granddaddy some time ago. Lightning immediately killed one right after the sale. He said he went to Paw, thinking that he might replace the loss. "Granddaddy, lightning killed one of my new heifers that I bought from you." Granddaddy just smiled at him, "Them that don't have 'em, don't lose 'em." Wes said he never once offered to replace the loss. I expect this was Wes' first lesson in Agricultural Economics 101.

But back to the cow huntin': we'd work several days or a couple of weeks at a time in the same daily routine. We'd go get the herd early, drive them into the pens, and sort them into separate groups of heifers, calves, cows, and bulls. The total number of cattle varied but was usually 300 to 400 head, as many as could be worked in a day. Occasionally, as I said, we'd get rained out and delayed, having to keep some cattle over night in little pastures that we called "traps". There they could rest, eat a bit and drink. But the idea was to work all the age groups and return the cattle to the pasture by dark. At that stage they might easily be rotated to another or better pasture. Sonny, Paw or Hubert opened the gates all the way back to the new destination. That way, it only took one or two men to take them back while the rest of the men rode to collect another group. The cattle had a tendency to resist being moved away from familiar surroundings but easily went back to them.

There were groups of "culls" and "sicks" to set aside for sale or treatment. Some of the cows in the cull group were exceptionally fat, either from overfeeding or from barrenness. It requires a tremendous amount of energy and protein to complete a pregnancy. When these barren cows didn't have the burden of "growing a calf," the body naturally restored condition. The unusually thin cows were generally wormy, sick, old or toothless.

Mammyin' up calves, Sortin' and the Art of Cowboy Cursing

"Truly ordinary people doing extraordinary things…"
-Baxter Black, D.V.M.

I was greatly impressed by the cowboy skill of "mammying up calves." Some men were better at this than others and it had more to do with observation than with education. They memorized cows and their calves or other individual cattle by body type, color and markings, joint and muscle conformation, or some outstanding event or temperament trait. During the confusion of gathering and moving to new pastures, calves could get separated from their mamas. The men could remember them as a pair, sometimes from a week or two back. They could spot the correct ones and reunite them, "mammyed-up", as Partner called it. Roping came in handy. I never was good at roping—I didn't have to be—I had Hubert and Ephraim. Remember, "If you own a dog you don't have to do tha' barkin'". I was good at coming up behind a caught cow and dropping a rope on her horns, but that skill was never much in demand. I also thought pen-sorting was a special talent. You'd sit on a board seat along a narrow alleyway with a gate handle in each hand. As the cattle ran down the alley, someone would call out the destination of the individual cow or small group: "cutbacks", "keepers", "calves", "bulls", "sicks", "sellers", "steers" or "heifers".

You manned a three-way cut: for example, you would direct them to the right side pen, the left side pen or under you, down the alleyway to a pen at the end. Things could get rather tense when two or three that needed to go to separate pens all crowded in the same area at the same time. It took considerable skill and experience to anticipate this wreck-in-the-making. If one got by the cut gate, and headed to the wrong gate, we'd have to shut everything down, turn everybody around and head them back. Then the whole thing would have to start all over. Again, this skill did not necessarily require high levels of education or intelligence, but it did require cow sense.

Cow sense was the understanding of cattle behavior and the ability to anticipate their reactions. It developed with experience or it sometimes came by temperament or, I suspected, even genetics. A few cows running over you a time or two usually helped in the learning curve. Paw said that Sonny was highly intelligent but he didn't have natural cow sense; he was more analytical. I didn't see it at first, thinking Paw was mistaken in this assessment. He said Wes, Sonny's son, had this cattle sense. Looking back, I think it is a matter of opportunity, intense interest, and powers of observation that develops this ability. I doubt a tenured Harvard professor could master the skills these Crackers took for granted.

Intelligence and coordination were assets in working cattle, but even a cowman who'd had no formal schooling could perform the task of "mammyin' up" quite efficiently if he had cow sense. I heard that some of the old Cracker cowboys couldn't count, but amid 400 head, they remembered an individual cow as being the mother of a particular calf. I heard tell of a Brighton man (Florida, not England) who could not count beyond ten. He'd work in "tens" through the cutting chute and made a mark on the post with his pocketknife when ten head had gone through. When asked how many, he'd say, "Four marks and 3 head." This meant 43 head. One day they had a real gate wreck and a whole bunch exploded in on him. He was overwhelmed. They heard him cry, "Eight…, nine…, ten…, ten…, ten…, cut 'em off…, ten.., Ten…, CUT 'EM OFF, BOYS!, ten, Ten, TEN!…DAMMIT! HELP ME, BOYS!"

Cursing was also an asset in the pens, communicating frustration and aggravation. It was highly effective when used with precision. Someone once said, "Profanity is the attempt of a lazy and feeble mind to express itself forcefully." I never really learned how to do it well. Most of the words they used were mild by today's standards. You can hear a lot worse in the fifth grade today. There was an invisible line that no one crossed and no one discussed it much.

I do know that when ladies came around to bring water, serve dinner or to watch the show, conversation cleaned up fast. It was an unspoken policy to watch your mouth when ladies were present. In general, I don't remember much bad language at all. I have reflected on this and I think it had to do with the quality of people who were hired there, a reflection of the characters of Paw and Sonny. I just don't remember anyone with a really bad cursing habit lasting long there. They didn't come back. They weren't asked to come back, I guess.

The worst thing we said was something like, "That damned ol' speckled bull liked to have kilt my horse back there." To tell the truth, that burnt-faced, speckled-necked Brahma bull of incestuous parentage was homicidally mean. We showed great verbal restraint in saying only that about him because he was worth a lot more cussin' than that. We sold him, which I thought was a good management decision. He didn't come back either. Hubert said, "He's crazier than ah outhouse rat." Only Hubert used a common term of German origin for "out-". I pictured a rat trapped in a dark outhouse, suddenly exposed to stark light as the door was abruptly opened—vivid. This phrase can be used to describe maniacally aggressive dogs and cats. Years later, while I was practicing veterinary medicine, on some permanent medical records, I abbreviated it as "CTAOR." One never knew when a client would read the records or if some clinician at the University of Florida would review the case. I wonder what they thought when they got to the "CTAOR" abbreviation. They might say, "What does this mean? I don't remember reading this in the literature. Who is this guy, anyway? What's his telephone number?"

Dr Frank Platt, our veterinarian, told me of a Cracker that worked at the Mormon owned and operated Desseret Ranch near Kenansville. He said there was a man named Lightsey that day-worked for them. ("Day-workin'" was the term used for a temporarily hired cowboy, working on a day-to-day basis.) There were several distinct properties at that time, each run by a Mormon foreman, while many of the cowboys, hired regulars and day-workers, were not of the Mormon persuasion.

Well Mr. Lightsey, in the heat of cattle handling reverted to the common cowboy language. He'd curse the cattle calling them by various colorful but profane words and descriptions. "Step up, you pig-eyed (*expletive deleted*)", "Go ahead, you silly son of a (*expletive deleted*), "Get on outa here, you snotty nosed (*compound expletive deleted*)", "You puzzle-gutted, wall-eyed (*expletive deleted*)" and other diverse but common variations. After a bit the foreman came over, courteously telling him, "Mr. Lightsey, we don't curse on this place. I'd appreciate it if you'd cut it out." This made him a little tight-jawed, but he cooled off the blistering language. As the men were packing their gear to leave, loading horses, gear, trailers and personal effects, Mr. Lightsey reflected, "Ya know…I worked cattle all my life and I didn't know you could do it without cussin' 'em…"

I Believe He's Better Help in the Cow Pens

"I've been to two county fairs and a goat ropin' an' I ain't never seen nuthin' like this."
-William R. Dudley, Jr., DVM -(From, *Dr. Strangelove*)

COW PENS work was intense but easier for me to pick up.

After gathering a herd and enclosing them in a pen, we'd secure our horses in some mottled shade of a pine tree or in a nearby pasture with bridles removed and hung over the saddle horn. They could wander around, eat grass or drink. Or they'd relax, "kick it into neutral" so to speak, half asleep in a three-legged stance, tail-switching at the multitudes of biting flies. It had to be an individual that was easy to catch. Green horses, stallions or ones that were just plum cantankerous were tied. Loose horses would sometimes pair up, stand head-to-tail, mutually tail-switching to scatter the flies off the other's face.

The group would have a few altercations among themselves, settling the issue of who was boss. Some appeared to be asleep but could instantaneously return to full awareness. You quickly learned not to approach one in this head-drooped, three-legged stance without warning. Calling the horse's name or a soft greeting did the trick, avoiding a sudden bone-jarring kick. I guess that is where I learned to talk to them; it settled them some. The head would snap up and ears would go on full alert. They'd move their rumps to one side a step or two, turn their heads toward us, roll their eyes, and snort-blow. Most were as tame as yard dogs, but some were a little saucy.

Horses aren't nearly as dumb as many say they are; however, they do think differently. A horse having an unpleasant experience with a particular person will remember that its entire life. This is common with veterinarians. One will inadvertently mishandle an animal, unconsciously communicating his fear, while another who understands horses has little trouble. The horse remembers a bad experience for many years. I learned the most vulnerable place on a horse was the flank. Some instinctive knowledge makes them generally wary of injury to that area. As the cowboys would say it, "Ya better watch yerself when ya goose him in the flank; he's touchus…"

The men usually dismounted to run cattle into the sorting pens on foot, but there were some places where the cowboys never got off their horses. They wouldn't even dismount to cross the pens to borrow a match. This wasn't common for us in our ranch corrals. The only exceptions were when we were handling rank bulls or really aggressive cattle. But generally, the cattle there weren't that wild and the men weren't that lazy.

Then we'd gather in the cow pens for a little conference where we'd get assignments. The first day was usually the only such discussion, but as the weeks wore on and we became aware of the big picture, changes might be made to speed things up. Everyone eventually grasped where he could contribute the best. The foreman or crew boss, who had efficiency in mind, was thinking days in advance. He knew how many head would be worked every day, what the cattle needed, the time of the year, the temperament of the cattle, the water situation and pasture grass condition. He knew the cost of "assling around" (i.e., lackadaisical work habits). He knew who was best at a particular task, who'd be vulnerable to injury and whom he could trust. A good crew boss was aware of all the small and large differences in pens, breeds, herds and crews. They all had their own variables and he could hone efficiency with occasional adjustments.

A good plan was to assign day-workers to the green ones, so the novice would get the idea. These short-term cowboys usually knew their business and could take the place of two or three green horns, especially with a trained cow dog backing them up. Some of these dogs were excellent help in the pens, as well as out cow hunting. They'd move cattle in the crowding pens, watch for the outlaws that came after a man, then bolt after the aggressor. The foremen didn't like uncontrolled dogs in the pens because of the confusion they caused. These could be told to "Go lay down!" and would disappear until called back.

But the best pens dog I ever saw was a Blue Heeler named, "Boss" Lowe. He'd sit beside me at the tail gate and watch. If a cow didn't step up when the tail gate opened, he'd run up, turn his head sideways, stick it between the boards and nip her in the flank. This was accomplished in a split-second. She'd get the hint and move up without much fuss. If the head catch gate opened and she stood there wondering if she ought to go through, Boss would reach up and nip her—expertly making up her mind for her. It got so the dog read my mind (or body language). Just for fun one day, I indicated to his owner Russell, "Watch this," and pointed at a stalled cow. On cue, as predicted, Boss immediately jumped to goose her up. Russell commented, "Well, that's good, but whutever you do, don't brag on 'im, He'll want to know where to send you his bill…"

At our ranch, the first day's meeting might sound like this: "Luther, you and Partner bring 'um in. Tie yer horses out in the trap and keep the pens loaded. Keep 'um coming to Clifford. I'll run the cut gates (the circular area in the center of the pens where cattle could be sorted or gate-cut in two, three or more directions into pens designated for calves, cows, bulls, etc.) Lonnie and Debo will run the chute; Debo, yer on the head-catch; Lonnie, you squeeze 'um and put the fly dope on 'um; DeRoy, you and Hiard run 'um down the alley and run tha back gate; one of you vaccinate. Debo, you deworm and read me the ear tags. I'll ear-mark an' brand any who need it. Y'all watch the hopper gate; it sticks. There're a couple of outlaws in this bunch. That ol' banana-horned Charolais bull and the red cow with the bicycle horns will ruin yer day if you crowd 'um. When she comes in, be sure an' tip her horns…so she'll not gut sumbody. Y'all put the dogs in the cow trailer. It's supposed to rain this afternoon so we need to titen up. Don't use tha hot-shots unless it absolutely necessary; we don't need any of 'um shook up…When we finish, put the cutbacks (cattle destined for sale) in the hammock pasture. The rest go back in the same pasture wher' we gathered 'em. Put tha' bulls out in the bull pasture."

And so it would begin.

From the time we closed the gates behind the first group until we finished, it was choreographed chaos. We established a working rhythm that set us in our own little worlds, each contributing to the whole. Gates slammed; cattle snorted and circled around, while dust (or mud) filled the air. A "Hah!" or "Hey!" would keep the jumpy animals moving down the alleyways. The chute would reverberate with a loud "Clang!" as a cow hit it, intense enough to cause hearing damage, indicating that the chute work had begun. The head catch slammed down to keep her from backing out, the tail gate was closed simultaneously and the sides squeezed in to keep her immobile. You could feel the vibration in the soles of your feet. We'd brand or mark her, check for dental wear, vaccinate her, do parasite control (de-worm, de-fluke and fly dip), and treat any ailments or diseases. We weighed cattle destined for sale and performed surgeries such as tipping, amputating or shortening horns. Determined by her age, brand and the time of year, she was palpated for pregnancy.

The term, "de-fluking" refers to the removal of a liver parasite found in wetland pastures. The Crackers called it, "flukin'" or "fluked," as in, "Did y'all fluke them cattle?" It meant, "Have y'all treated these cattle for <u>Fasciola hepatica</u> parasitism by giving the proper medicine for the removal of the nematode parasite found in the bovine liver?" (If I'd said that in the pens, they'd have looked at me a little fishy-eyed, and replied, "You ain't from around here, are ya?")

Meanwhile, the men out in the pens were loading more into the long chute and sorting them to keep the line moving. Only the younger keeper heifers were branded with a simple ranch brand. The less desirable heifers, along with steers, were destined for the market. Later, we started to identify individuals with branded numbers so we could keep performance records. The fluke medicine was hexa-chlorbenzathine, as I recall. It has been so long ago and the drug is so outdated, I can't remember if that is the correct name. We usually called it, "hex". Today's medications for liver flukes and intestinal parasites are much improved and less toxic to the animal, have fewer side effects and are much more effective. The de-wormer we used then was called phenothiazine. It was only about 45% effective in the removing of intestinal parasites, but that rate, along with good grass, was enough to give them an edge in survival, even growth. I remember that pasty green phenothiazine would blister your skin. You looked like a Midwestern tourist that had fallen asleep on the beach wherever it touched your face. Creosote from treated fence posts would give the same tourist sunburn.

The last thing for the adult cattle was the tick and fly treatment. If we'd held the mamas separately, while working their babies, we'd run the bigger calves through the dip vat with the adults. The little gals and fellas could get enough residues on them when they nursed their mamas. Turning them out also avoided their being hurt in the scramble. Preparing for this last activity involved charging up the dip vat with fresh chemicals and running the cattle into the treated water and out the shallow end. It was like a long narrow swimming pool. After dipping, the cows were put out in a holding pasture or trap.

The bulls were worked somewhat the same way, but it was a little more dangerous with them. In the fall, they were separated from the cows. It would sometimes take two men to hold their heads still while another administered the drench. The old restraining chutes where we held the cattle for treatments were like some wicked medieval devices. You could get knocked silly by the tailgates and head-catch mechanisms. We'd tape foam rubber pads on the protruding joints that so that when it hit you, it wouldn't slash your skin.

It took a crew of about eight to twelve men to work the cattle efficiently those days: a vaccinator, a drencher, a head-catch man, a squeeze man, a tail-gate man, a hot brander, a harasser (a man that "worrys" the cattle to move them toward the chute in an alleyway), one or two to get them into a small pen connected to the alleyway and a couple to work the outside pens to keep herding the cattle into the sorting pens. All that has changed today—for the better I might add. Cattle chutes now are hydraulically operated. One man can catch the cow, squeeze her up, restrain the head and shut the back door. He can then vaccinate, de-worm, de-fluke, brand, record identification numbers and make decisions about where she goes. (And, yes, Ethyl, there are computers in cow pens these days…) Many pens are designed to require only one or two men to bring them in and sort into groups. It usually takes a hassling to get them into the sorting pens. So, twelve men are reduced to about 3 or 4 by these modern systems.

Working the calves was a dramatic experience. Once the adults were done and turned out to rest, the calves were brought around for sorting into groups or we worked them as a mixed group. Each team of men had particular jobs. When we only did vaccinations, branding and marking, the pen might be filled with 300 calves, all crowded together in the corners. They'd get hot, frightened and panicky. All ages and sizes commingled together. The little ones, the youngest, would be picked off first and moved out to another pen when we could so they wouldn't get trampled in the organized turmoil.

One man was the "leg catcher." He had a sidekick (no pun intended) who stayed close to him as extra muscle, providing a supporting pair of hands to handle the big calves. The leg catcher was responsible for choosing the calf to be caught. The trick was to approach a calf where he couldn't see you and shove yourself in close to him. A kick from 2-3 feet away can sure ruin your day, but if he kicks you from very close up, it doesn't hurt so much. This was a hard thing to learn with horses, too. A horse can break your leg from a distance but up close, he could only shove you. You'd end up with only a hematoma, contusion, abrasions and multiple bruises or lacerations from landing on the piled-up galvanized roofing near the horse barn—instead of a hospital visit.

The best way to hand-catch a calf in a group was to approach the group slowly, pick out your target and then lunge at it. The best choices were the ones with their heads down among the tightly packed bodies. They couldn't see you coming. Next, was to pick up his back leg and slide your grip down below the hock. Having a rear leg grabbed was quite unsettling for the calf. It kicked and lunged, trying to shake you off; sometimes it succeeded and you'd have to start over. More than a few times one would slip the grip and pop-kick us on the knee with a bone-jarring "Whack!"

Usually the meatiest man did this—one with lots of chest muscle. But us skinny ones were expected to take our turns. Even Hubert's young boys tried it, as skinny as they were, like earth worms with their guts slung out. Reeny was too young at the time, but I remember when she grew older she worked in the pens like one of the men…and she was a whole lot purtier.

The leg-catcher immediately grabbed the animal's back leg while another, if necessary, helped hold the big ones. He slipped in beside the calf, leaned over to catch the flank fold of skin in front of the back leg along with a front leg, and heaved the whole calf off the ground with his knee. It was just like lifting an eighty-pound bale of hay. The calf "cha-lunked" to the ground and another man jumped on its head, grabbing the front leg. He put his knee on the hopefully outstretched neck at the shoulder and fold-pulled the upper front leg back to the calf's side and chest. His weight prevented the calf from rolling upright. We worked the smaller, younger calves first, leaving the older, larger, ranker ones till later. The idea was to get the little ones out of the way, to keep them from injury.

The bigger calves were quicker and more experienced and could better evade our many attempts at catching them. So we, by the process of elimination, pared down to the mean, tough, heavy calves that were looking for trouble and it was usually just about dark, when we were nearly worn out.

Sometimes it took three or four men to hold a big calf down. We also had to think about keeping our butts out of the way of the brander and the vaccinator.

Maybe I ought to take another rabbit trail here: the term ear marking refers to the age old practice of cutting or trimming of cattle's ears for identification.

Ears were cropped with a mark designating ownership for each ranch or for a particular member of the family. There were splits, double splits, crops, swallow forks, sharps ("sharpees"), upper-bits, under-bits, as well as creative combinations and doublings. Descriptive terms such as steeple- or swallow fork, over- or under slope, over- and under bit, single or double split, crops, and many others. Each have an identifying characteristic. The swallow fork showed a neat triangular portion removed, resulting in a missing wedge-like shape to the ear. A "sharpee" was a term used for the literal sharpening of the ear to a distal point. A foreman might tell the earmarker, "Put a swallow fork right and a crop-split left." The various combinations and variations were used to make the animal easily identifiable. It took a very sharp knife and a steady hand. The ear-marker was continuously sharpening his knife with a pocket stone.

"Brammers," had huge ears, making ear marking very easy to read from a distance. The crop mark was usually reserved for the animal destined for sale to slaughter though in some states it is an illegal mark since it removes identification. Examples are shown below. (An amazing void exists in the literature showing Cracker ear marks, so I made my own examples.)

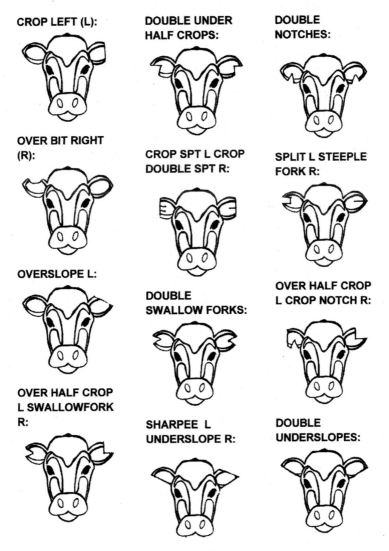

CROP LEFT (L):

DOUBLE UNDER HALF CROPS:

DOUBLE NOTCHES:

OVER BIT RIGHT (R):

CROP SPT L CROP DOUBLE SPT R:

SPLIT L STEEPLE FORK R:

OVERSLOPE L:

DOUBLE SWALLOW FORKS:

OVER HALF CROP L CROP NOTCH R:

OVER HALF CROP L SWALLOWFORK R:

SHARPEE L UNDERSLOPE R:

DOUBLE UNDERSLOPES:

Examples of Ear Marks

Of course, any ear mark could be mangled by the cow dogs when the cattle went after a horse and rider. Imagine the canine teeth grabbing an ear and the cow's violence redirected toward the dog. When the dog was slung off, the teeth stripped out two parallel tear-cuts, looking like an odd "double split" ear mark. This sounds rough to those who've never been chased and caught by a killer bull or cow. When we saw a Brahma bull with a mangled ear push his way to the edge of a tightly bunched herd, it meant to get out of his way; he'd eat your sack lunch...

Though still practiced in some areas, the earmark has been mostly replaced by plastic identification tags containing information about the animal; i.e., ID number, age, group, significant dates, pregnancy status, etc. are recorded on the tag. Some tags come in packages of various colors, sequential numbers and/or lettering and some are designed to allow the owner to write his own information.

A leg catcher, a support man, a head and shoulder man on the big ones, an ear marker, a vaccinator, a lay surgeon, a de-horner and a brander were needed for this calf working fun-in-the-sun. The catchers and holders would wear out from exertion and the heat. So a rested team of two or three leg catchers and holders waited in the background under a hot sun, arms folded and one boot cocked on the fence board. If there was shade, you took advantage of it while you rested. You kept catching and working until you started losing your grip or got dehydrated. Then a new team spelled you. With all limbs aching, you could amble over, out of the way, and get a badly needed drink of water. Though it ever tasted of sulfur, it was good.

Sometimes two teams worked simultaneously. This kept the branders, ear-markers and castrator/vaccinators busy. Indelibly imprinted on my mind are the smells of churned up dirt, fresh manure (which really doesn't smell that bad), bawling calves, burning literd wood and oak fires, the oppressive heat and annoying flies. Many times the flies left the freshly dipped cattle, looking for a new host, and would swarm in on a man, settling on his back. They'd bite, too.

Later, portable propane tanks provided the fuel for heating the brands. I thought it interesting that many old timers added wood to the fire-pot where the blast of propane flame heated the brands. You would see oak wood and small chunks of literd there. I think to them it was a subconscious reminder of the old days. In a good propane brand heater there was no need for wood. Apparently in their minds, you couldn't brand without the smell of wood smoke. I remember working near these branding fires, and later the propane heaters. The smell of burnt hair and smoke was in the air. There is no other smell like that of brand smoke. Once experienced, it's not soon forgotten. Gloves were a necessity to keep from burning our hands on the brand handles. Branding was over quickly, much quicker than a tattoo and was permanent identification.

It was a whirlwind of activity. Paw warned, "Look around you every now and then. A lotta problems can be headed off if you stay aware of whut's happenin' in the rest of the pens." The Cracker cowboys knew this instinctively. A yelled warning meant you better get your head up and see what was coming your way. The sharp sound of breaking boards was another signal. Once I'd heard the "cha-lack" of boards breaking in the cow pens, I've never forgotten it. It was more often than not followed by, "Hold up a minute! We gotta breakdown!" Then you'd hear the sound of a hammer framming nails.

Frantic cows and mean bulls tried break-outs. The worst wrecks occurred when an animal tried to jump a fence and caught a hind leg in between the top two boards. If the boards were strong, the full weight of the escapee would be transferred to the leg. We'd have to stop all operations, gather men, horses, ropes and other gear to get the thrashing animal out of trouble. We'd rope her and tie the rope to a saddle horn. While one man had his horse pulling, we'd muscle her up and back into the pens. At times, the animal was so big and the boards so strong, the only way we could free a cow would be to saw or remove some boards to untangle legs. Surprisingly, very few broke their legs in this way—it was rare. I was amazed that they all didn't break their legs, but these cattle were tough as nails.

Cattle and horses were not the only ones that could get injured. Side panels on the catch chute were designed to open to give access to the side of the animal for branding, vaccinations or identification of number brands. When a rank one hit the chute, some of the panels could pop loose and slam a careless by-stander. A cow hitting a chute when the crew wasn't ready for the catch could knock a side panel out as fast as shot from cannons. These old chutes had many parts that jutted out some one to two feet. Depending on the design of the working chute, some of these protrusions were head level, sometimes just above the brim of one's hat. All it took was one or two hits to teach a fella to keep his body clear of the flying panels and levers. The old front clamp-down levers at the head catch stuck out to allow leverage for the operator. If it was carelessly held, a cow could hit the gate and pop the handle up at break-neck speed—literally. If your face or chin was in the way, it would, as the cowboys would say, "outten yer lights." More than one cowboy has had cuts, bruises or fractured bones from these chutes. I am surprised that many haven't been killed.

In spite of the real danger, the men loved their work. If a cowboy escaped being hurt around the horses or equipment, he was subject to being gored, mashed, butted, wallered, trampled, kicked or stepped on by the cattle. Shoot, some of these injuries were caused by men running over each other. You could lose a finger or tooth (or three), get knocked-down, -blind, -silly or -out, and suffer a variety of broken bones from the restraint chutes. Some of the most unimaginable colors could come out in the bruises: green, yellow, blue, red, and black. It amazed me that the Cracker men kept coming back to work. They never paid it much mind.

I remember hurting my foot later in the summer during a water skiing lesson. It was too sore to run on, much less climb a fence, but I went to work, too proud to stay home. I was a hazer that day. A white heifer who didn't like the way things were going, turned back straight for me. I hobbled toward the fence thinking to climb it before I realized that there was no way I could manage with a sore foot. So I turned to face the heifer, hoping she would just try to bluff me and dodge away at the last second. She didn't. She came right on, bellowing in my face, butting me down, slobbering on me and wallering me in the dirt. Somehow, I got out of that situation, just barely, with only some skin and my pride bruised. Hubert seemed amused by my adventure, "When that cow was maulin' you, you kinda sounded like a girl." I don't remember how I sounded—I was too busy at the moment.

But I learned many lessons from these Crackers. I am grateful for the protection they gave me and the others. More than once, someone would grab a fella's arm, pulling (or pushing) him back from harm.

Each of the health and management procedures in the catch chute, with the exception of dipping or spraying the groups, took from thirty seconds to nearly a minute. Yes, Myrtle, when the crew was moving like an oiled sewing machine, cattle were worked at rates of fifty to one hundred head an hour. This rate was reduced by bull or cow attacks, fence tear-ups and breakouts, chute breakdowns and "wrecks," where a man or horse was injured or cattle were jammed in a gate or turned upside-down in the passage leading to the catch chute. At times, there were pile-ups like autos wrecked in a fog bank. The cattle would try some neat tricks and we learned to expect the unexpected. If there was a weak spot in the fences, they'd find it or make one. Bulls jumped the gates and fences, tearing top boards off the fence. Broken-down gates allowed unworked cattle to rejoin the finished cattle. As a result, the men had to not only repair the gate, but also re-sort the groups.

Hubert and Sonny usually had some nails and tools stored in the pens. If there was a sizable hole in the fence and there were no supplies to repair it, the men would make a panel of woven palm fronds, an ersatz repair of sorts. It was pure bluff and camouflage, one a drunken bumblebee could knock down.

An isolated animal might frantically and repeatedly try to escape, but mixing her with a group usually helped calm her. I've seen grown men mill around for a half-hour looking for one nail to hold up a board with the cattle lowing all around them. They used to say that a good veterinarian carries a few good nails and wire in the truck.

But all in all, with good crews, cow pens work generally went smoothly and injuries were rare.

We had all kinds of fun in the mud, dust, blood, sweat, pain and fatigue. Burning heat, humidity and the clouds of flies seeking new hosts were the price of admission. Men came back every day—bruises, soreness and all. I had to open my hands slowly in the mornings, creating ripples of forearm tenderness. Stretching was a real adventure. But in a day or two, it wasn't near as bad as it was the first day. The men were hardened, toughened, skilled and gritty. They were a good role model for me. I suppose it was the challenge of it that attracted us—a game of sorts. Yes, it was hard, dangerous work but especially valuable for me as a young man of low confidence. It got into my blood. The cow pens work formed a loyal and lasting camaraderie among us and gave each of us an immense sense of accomplishment.

If I had to summarize cow pens work, I'd have to say it was hours of boring, repetitive, tedious, stressful physical work, interrupted by episodes of chaotic terror and frenzied excitement—very much like motherhood…

Saddle Weary but Content

WHEN memories creep into my consciousness like soft rain showers in the mountains, many colorful stories and noteworthy Florida Crackers come to mind. After finishing those hard days in the cow pens I remember the times heading home in the saddle after dark. Every herd that was worked had to be put back in its home pasture or rotated to a new one. After the day's activities we rode to the barn, usually slumped in the saddle as spent riders riding spent horses, mostly lost in our own thoughts. There wasn't much conversation, just some quiet comments from time to time or a muffled chuckle. Then a story would follow about some happening out in a particular pasture or about some notable individual. The cowboys discussed people and places, embellishing wherever it was deemed appropriate. Every now and then we spooked an armadillo or fox out for an evening meal, or a deer snorting an alarm.

Morgan Bonaparte "Bone" Mizell was a character worthy of local lore. He definitely was surrounded by myth, legend and embellishment as time moved on. Jim Bob Tinsley's book, *Florida Cow Hunter: The Life and Times of Bone Mizell* gives some accounts of this colorful legendary Florida Cracker.

Paw had a version of the story that I'm sure has been changed over the years, but I enjoyed it anyway. A good friend of Bone's had died and was buried near the outskirts of town. (I think Paw said the friend's name was John Underhill.) Not long after Underhill's death, another young man came to Tater Hill to soak up the color and flavor of a real Florida outlaw town. This young man was from New Orleans and from the descriptions given by contemporary sources had a debilitating disease. The man took up with Bone and his crowd—following them everywhere and enjoying them no end. Well, the young man died soon afterwards and Bone buried him near the grave of his good friend. It wasn't long before a stranger arrived, a detective of sorts, looking for the young man. He had tracked him to Arcadia. Upon learning that the boy had died and been buried, the family sent money to exhume the body to transfer it to New Orleans for re-burial in the ancestral plot.

Now Bone knew which grave was his, but the story goes that he pointed out his friend's grave instead. The casket was dug up and carefully placed on the wagon. As the buckboard left the grave site, heading for the train station, Bone remarked that as his friend hadn't been anywhere much and had never taken a train ride, this was a chance for him to travel all the way to New Orleans. After a bit, Bone's eyes twinkled. He commented, "Boys, when Resurrection Day comes, he's gonna raise up, look around and say, 'Ou-u-u Wee! Ain't Arcadia growed!'"

Paw told about the times when the screwworms infested Florida cattle as well as the wildlife. Screwworms are the larval stage of a fly, whose scientific name I forget (I knew it once "The mark of an educated man is: He knows the answer, he just can't think of it.") The fly still survives in Mexico and Central and South America. Disease control officials are constantly on guard against re-introduction of them into this country. Texas, New Mexico and Arizona are the battlegrounds today. The adult worm lays eggs in an open sore or wound or the navels of newborn calves. In the forties, Florida had a considerable problem with this parasite. Just about every new calf would have a screwworm infection. Specifically, infestation led to infection and the odor was horrible from the necrotic mass of larvae. They applied, as prevention and treatment, a sticky tar and insecticide product, "screwworm paste" or "dope". I can smell it today. The product had to be sticky to keep attached to the wet wounds.

I mention this to relate what Paw told about a cowboy he had hired during the screwworm days in Florida. He said he happened to look out in the marsh, spotting the man's horse standing at a three-legged rest near some lone palm trees. He thought this odd, since it was about 3:00 in the afternoon. Why would an experienced cowboy be off his horse when he would ordinarily be out looking for newborn calves to doctor with screwworm paste? Had the man been thrown? Was he injured? He became a little concerned, and drove his Jeep out in the marsh toward the horse. Well, the wind was in his face, the sound of the Jeep engine was muffled, so the fella couldn't hear him coming. As Paw approached the horse, which was unconcerned at his approach, the man raised up from his nap in the shade of a palm, stood up, stretched, yawned and loudly called out, "Iny you calves want yer navels doctored, come on up here." Apparently, the fella had been asleep since noon. This is typical Cracker humor.

Partner was the tale-teller and could be inspired by the rambling conversations. He related one that I remember: "One time on the prairie I was lookin' for cattle. It was ah hot, miserable day. I heard something coming through the brush. I happened to be comin' around the edge of a big palmetto patch, up next to ah big shallow pond. Me and Pied were just amblin along, about half asleep, when this boogery sound came out tha patch. Tha blamed palmetto fans swizzled back an forth; whatever it wuz, wuz comin after me and Pied hard! Wellsir, I sez to myself, 'I best hang a spur in Pied's flank to wake him up some', but Pied wuz way aheadah me. He woke withah jump—just before the spur connected and before this thing got to us. I thinks to myself, 'It must a big hog, a rank bull, a bear, a bull gator or mean cow or somethin big anyways…' I didn't take a lotta time to figure on it much since Pied wuz already boogered about the whole situation. One quick jouge to the left an' we wuz clear of tha' palmettos—jus' in time tah see it was a humongous mosquito comin' at us! Tha thing wuz huge! Its wings had a span over twenty feet! Tha bill on it looked like a long fence post."

Now that everyone was interested, he continued. "Pied decided to take the bit in his teeth an pulled out for tha open prairie. I 'spect he wuz wide open in 'bout thirty feet. Tha danged thing took to us an' come right in behind Pied. It was butt over teakettle for ah time. I headed Ol' Pied for a pine thicket that wuz near, thinkin', I guess, that if I could sail in amongst it, it'd slow the mosquito down some. I'd observed that it couldn't turn real good. So into tha trees we went, darting left and right, circling here and there; the mosquito was havin' a devil of a time trying to keep up. We'd dart to the left and the mosquito would fly past us, makin' a wide turn to git back on our trail."

It was quiet by this time. All eyes and ears concentrated on him. He paused for several seconds, then went on with the story. "Well Ol' Pied hadda a hard mornin' an' he begun to slow down some. The mosquito must hav' been encouraged since he kept comin'! Now I'm not noted for thinkin' too deep on matters, but I figured I better cum up with an idea and I mean quick! Pied wuz about to give out. It cum to me like a dream: 'Why not git this critter hung up in the trees?' So off we went deeper inta tha thickest strand of pines I could see. Pied seemed to trust me, after all, it wuz a lot better than whut he had in mind, which wuz to buck me off an' high-tail it for home."

Partner took another dramatic pause for effect. During the moments, all we could hear was the night sounds of quail locating each other, bull bats warming up their hum-calls and varmints scurrying for cover. A horse snorted. Somebody's saddle had squeaking leathers and Thunder's bit chain was jingling. Partner continued.

"Into the pines we went. In and out of the thicket we went, circlin', dartin', dodgin', and suckin' back here and there, tryin' to confuse or wear out the mosquito. I even turned my hat and shirt backwards to make the thing think I wuz goin' in the opposite direction...Nothin' was workin'... Y'all'll never guess whut happened...Durin' one of the darts, the mosquito made a mistake; he plunged his bill into a pine tree. Before he could pull it out, I jumped off Pied, grabbed a litered knot and braded the bill over so's he couldn't pull it out. Well there wuz all kinds of commotion while the thing beat and frammed the dirt, shakin the tree', while tryin' to pull out his stuck beak. Me and Pied took a breather, watchin' the thing for a while. Finally, we went on back to cow huntin'."

By this time somebody said, "Now Partner...Are you sure about all this? It sounds purty hard to swaller..." Partner chuckled and said, "Why yes, that's ezzactly how it happened. Six months later, I went back by that pine tree and there wuz enough bones left to build a set of cow pens."

About Florida Crackers

"I am of the opinion that "Southern" and "Cracker" had similar roots, and I may have stumbled on the basis. The Cracker spirit originated in the character of the frontiersmen, the same spirit found in frontier Kentucky a hundred years before. As a boy reared in Kentucky I was around people of similar quality and attitude as Florida Crackers. This may be the reason I am so comfortable with them; I never had any difficulty in adjusting to their culture. They made me feel at home."
-HSJ

James Kirke Paulding, in *Westward Ho!* wrote regarding Kentucky frontiersmen:
"The result of their peculiar situation, habits, and modes of thinking has been a race of men uniting in a fearlessness of danger, a hardy spirit of enterprise, a power of supporting fatigues and privations, and an independence of thought which perhaps were never associated with the pursuits and acquirements of civilized life in any other country than the United States."

JUNIOR MILLS was one of the men that came to the ranch to work cattle. A true Florida Cracker, lean and tough, he had a craggy face and prominently pointed chin. His lower face was bronze but the top half of his head was white as a baby's butt. He talked a lot but was all business when it came to working. His horse was a common-looking little bay as I recall. Everybody there liked him. He liked grits, fried fat side-meat, rice and gravy and beans, also stewed swamp cabbage with tomatoes and fried fatback bacon chips. "Swamp cabbage" in rural Florida is the same thing as "hearts of palm" in New York City, only there's about a fifty-dollar difference in what you call it between here and there.

Junior said he once owned a horse that was bad to run away with you. He went on about how he tried to, in his words, "stop the stupid (*expletive deleted for obscure or illegitimate parentage*)". But he never was able to break him of it. He said one day he'd had enough of the aggravation. As the crazy horse pulled out at a mach-one gallop, the bit clamped in his teeth, Junior reached back in the saddle bags, pulled out his pistol, aimed and shot the beast square between the ears. "It dawned on me as I pulled the trigger that we were moving at a wide-open gallop, but it was too late. The horse's head went between his front legs and I sailed off into the palmettos." He paused and reflected, "Boys, don't never shoot a runnin' horse between the ears while you're ridin' him." I never found out if this was a tall tale or if it was true. Nobody else was there, so who knows? I never tried it either, but I am sure some sap did. You can see what the elderly Junior Mills looks like on the cover of Jon Kral's photography book *Cracker—Florida's Enduring Cowboys*.

Junior told about a cow crew that was working cattle, jawing about this and that. When some girls came up to watch. Well, all of a sudden, the pace picked up and everyone was snapping to their tasks with new resolve. The idea was, I guess, to impress the girls. Well, one old bull decided he might like it better outside the pens. He took a short run at the fence and leapt up over it. The top two boards crushed with that "cha-lack" sound that is unmistakable to the men who work in cow pens. He tilted over and fell off the fence on the far side, heading to parts of galaxies far, far away. One of the young men dove off the fence where he had climbed to see what was happening, jerked the slipknot on the reins, started the horse off, bouncing once on the ground like Roy Rogers and skip-whipped his body into the saddle. All this happened in a few split-seconds and he was ahead of all the other cowboys. As things developed, he had one great start on catching up to the bull. He uncoiled his rope at a full gallop, made a nice loop and twirled the rope over his head, just like a professional roper. As he got along beside the bull, he threw the loop, making a perfect toss. The only problem was that, once he had him in the loop, his saddle began to slide sideways. He slid more quickly than he ordinarily would have since the horse had panicked at this new roping technique, and had begun to buck violently. Junior said, "That's when the hair hit the cake."

The eager boy hit the dirt hard amid the palmettos, raised up in time to see his horse throw a fit, break off the saddle, kick to kill it and trot off in triumph. The bull never slowed down, dragging the man's saddle behind. The girls loved it. The men laughed so hard, they had to quit working for a time. The fella walked all the way back to the pens. He didn't say much for the rest of the day. I think he married one of the girls, however.

Years ago, Cracker cowboys went to camp for weeks or months while they worked cattle in communal cow pens. A few men carried with them what is called out west, "a war bag". It was a sack, such as a gunnysack, poke, potato sack, feed sack or hemp sack. In this war bag they would carry personal items: leather for saddle repairs, string, wire, nails and staples, maybe a hammer or staple puller, an extra knife, a magazine, a can of beans or other food items, an orange or two, and anything else they thought they would need in the woods. Sometimes the cow pens were so isolated you couldn't go home for supplies. A cow camp would be set up at some central location, usually near shade trees with available firewood and a water supply such as a creek or pond. Tents were rare. Tarpaulins or sheets of canvas served as some shelter for gear and from rain. Many of the men were skilled at making little water-shedding shelters from the cabbage palm fronds. They sometimes bathed in the creeks; clothes hung on bushes, boots askew on the bank. They wore their hats while bathing.

From these camps the men prowled the woods, locating cattle, moving them to communal pens or they bunched them up and worked them in the open. Once they'd "mammy'd up" the calves with their mothers, they cut out the calves from the herd, roped, marked and branded them, and turned them loose. I am sure that mistakes were made in branding and marking due to mistaken ownership. Hard feelings could boil up over it. But generally they were honest people.

The old Florida Cracker cowboys were not your stereotypical Western cowboys as seen in cinemas, all dressed in felt Stetson hats, flowing bandanas, chaps, bright pointy-toed boots with silver spurs, flashy shirts and tight jeans. In fact, a Cracker cowboy typically wore a raggedy straw cowboy hat, round-toed brogans (flat-heeled lace-up boots) with spurs and bib overalls. It has changed now. Crackers wear jeans, working cowboy boots, but many still wear their flea-bitten cowboy hats. Some even wear baseball hats now in the cow pens, so you can tell the difference between them and semi-truck drivers…

JACK PAGE hired on as one of the crew one fall. On one of the cow hunting trips in the woods, he found a sweet orange tree full of ripe oranges. He rode his horse up next to the tree and filled his partly unbuttoned shirt with them. He'd eat a few every now and then. Well, something happened with the cows and they all had to get serious. Jack took a hard tumble off his horse. Sonny found him wallowing and moaning on the ground. His horse was nearby. He called to Sonny, "Help me, Sonny. I've fallen and my guts are mashed out and they're rolling around inside my shirt. I'm hurt bad." He moaned as Sonny got off his horse and opened Jack's shirt. He said, "Dangit,

Jack—you ain't hurt—it's nothing but squashed oranges. Git up and let's go." That is not the only thing I heard about Jack and his affinity for fruit…

Jack loved guavas. He was working for John Olin Pearce, Sr. Mr. Pearce was a descendant of the Colonel Pearce that settled at Ft. Basinger, just a little ways northwest of Okeechobee. John Olin was a true Cracker, lean and tough. He was the stereotypical cowboy of the old west, but he was born and reared in Florida. He was flamboyant, colorful, loud, sanguine and wealthy, having made his money by shrewd land deals, appreciation and cattle ranching. He would have been a perfect character for a Louis L'Amour book. The Pearce outfit was working near a large marsh. Gathering cattle here could be tricky since there were boggy places and you could get scrubbed off your horse by one of the myrtle trees. Jack found a guava tree with mostly ripe guavas and proceeded to load up his shirt with them. Some might have been a little green, but he ate them anyway. As it happens at times in the course of cow huntin', there was a stampede. Simultaneously, Jack had an attack of lower gastrointestinal distress due to his consumption of excessive numbers of guavas. He just had to get off his horse and relieve himself. There was no cover; the only place was at the base of a myrtle tree, and he was short of time, so he squatted there in traditional fashion. John Olin rode up, shouting, "Jack! Can't you see that we're in a tight? We need help with these cattle, now!" John Olin rode off in a huff. Jack was already too committed to jump up and ride. When he could, he caught up with the crew, helping take the cattle to the pens some miles away. No one made mention of the episode.

The story continues. Later that week, on Saturday, as was the routine, the crew went to Padgett's Drugstore to get their paychecks. Located across the street from the old Southland Hotel, Padgett's Drugs was an old fashioned drug store with a soda counter, red-seated chrome stools and gaudy signs advertising some ice cream concoction. There was shelf upon of shelf of necessities like Epsom's Salts, Hadecol, blister paste, hemorrhoid cream, foot thrush medicine, iodine, hernia trusses and other necessities of the time. It had a medicinal smell. Madeline Padgett moved around among visitors when she was not filling soda and malted milk orders. She kept her ears open, too. She was rather abrupt at times, being a no nonsense type of gal. But she enjoyed people, was quick to laugh, and they enjoyed her. She knew most everyone by first name.

Mr. Pearce sat at the soda counter while writing paychecks for the men. Jack Page stood around but didn't hear his name called to get his check. Now, nothing went on at Padgett's that everyone didn't know about.

Madeline Padgett was a first rate clearinghouse of local gossip. I heard that a few hung back to see what would happen. Finally, after everyone had been paid, Jack was summoned to the soda counter. Mr. Pearce started a long dissertation about how a cow crew needed every man it had. He'd write a little on the check before him, pause, look up and begin another lesson on how a man needs to earn his pay when he works for someone. Jack stood there with his hat in his hands. Mr. Pearce would write a little and tell about how they were in a real tight spot, how they needed him to pull his own weight. He told him that he just thought that a man should be more conscientious in his duties. "Day workers need to earn their wages; this kind of thing can git a man fired…" he scolded Jack. After the long lecture, John Olin finally finished and signed the check he had been intermittently writing all along. Turning on the swivel seat, John Olin handed Jack's check to him, faintly smiling. When Jack looked at the check, Mr. John Olin Pearce had drawn a little cowboy squatting under a myrtle bush with his hat rocked back on his head and his britches down to the ankles. Jack showed it to the whooping by-standers. John Olin walked out without a word. Jack thought about keeping it for the fine artwork, but he needed the money. I wonder what the bank tellers thought when they cleared the check?

Jack's paycheck was not the only incident that John Olin pulled at Padgett's. Dr. Frank Platt, the veterinarian, sold him about 40 cases of medicine for de-worming his cattle herds. Things went on as usual until about 4 weeks later. John Olin called out to Frank across the store, "Dr. Platt…that damned ol' worm medicine you sold me ain't done a bit of good for my cattle." Dr. Platt look over with a quizzical expression, not knowing exactly what to say to this prominent cash-paying citizen. It didn't sound good in the heart of Gossip Central. "Do you know why that worm medicine didn't do no good, Dr. Platt?" Mr. Pearce continued loudly over the counters. Dr. Platt frowned, "No, Mr. Pearce. I don't know why it didn't work. It should have." John Olin smirked, "Well, I'll tell you exactly why it didn't work. It's still in the jugs in my garage where I unloaded it last month."

Paw said that Jack Page used to drive a cattle truck. He would get to the ranch around noon when the men gathered to eat rice and beans and fried meat. Of course, it was customary to ask a visitor to eat with them. Jack knew this and took every advantage of the ranch's hospitality. They had an old dog there named Rock. I think he was a true Florida Cur. He was probably about 90 pounds, big, tough, stocky and hard. Paw said he was a little mean. They could sic him on anything or anyone. Well, one day Jack pulled in just as everyone was heading in to the table. He was half-way to the bunk house when someone growled, "Ketch 'em, Rock." Rock did not take any time to consider the morals of the directive nor ponder universal truths, he just took off after Jack. Jack made it to a big post. He climbed up just as snapping jaws popped under his butt. They said they could hear him crying and moaning all the way to the house at the dinner table. He begged for someone to come call the dog off him. They all said that he really was more concerned about missing the meal than he was about the dog. He didn't test him, however.

Partner once flagged Jack down driving a cow truck, under a full head of steam with a heavy load of fat market cattle. Partner said it took Jack a quarter-mile to stop. When Partner finally came up to the cab with pungent burnt rubber and hot engine smells all around, he said. "Say, Jack, you got a match?" Partner learned new ways to use cuss words that day, too. Paw liked Jack. He laughed about Rock treeing him on the post.

RUDY ASHTON of Lorida, Florida (pronounced "Low-REE'-dah") was an old style Cracker. He wore bib overalls, denim jackets (in the winter), and brogans with heavy spurs to work cattle. One year as he attended the annual Lake Placid Rodeo (Florida, not New York), the younger men asked him to compete in steer roping. After much encouragement, aided by several sips from the whiskey flask he carried, he agreed. Well, there was nothing flashy about Rudy. He made the throw, catching the steer calf the first time. He got off his horse deliberately, approaching the steer like an angry bear. Rudy picked the whole animal off the ground, piled him in a stunned heap, and tied him in a knot that was a guarantee he'd never get loose. Rudy used what is called a "hatchet knot"—it'd take a hatchet to get the rope off the steer. To Rudy, time was not the issue.

In the process of tying, his whiskey bottle slipped out of his pocket. One of the flag judges, "Boy" McGown, toed the bottle over behind and away from Rudy, bent down and slipped in into his own pocket. Rudy finished the tie and rose up to a standing ovation. After acknowledging the applause he felt in the back pocket of his bib overalls for his bottle. Finding nothing he looked all around the churned-up ground. No bottle…He went back over to the tied steer, lifted it completely off the ground and walked around with it, kicking the dirt for the bottle. The audience went wild for they had seen the theft by Boy. So don't tell me a cowboy can't wear spurs with brogans. I think they awarded Rudy for the best show in steer roping. His prize was a half empty bottle of whiskey, handed to him after being swigged on by Boy McGown.

Rudy owned property around the northeastern shore of Lake Istopo-ka. In the sixties, he sold a few acres to a man who put in a RV trailer park. Someone commented, "Rudy, you sold some of yer land to them Yankees?" He just shook the wrinkle out of the newspaper he was reading there on the porch at the grocery and said, "Yeah an' they damshur know they've bin to ah sale." That tiny piece of land would be worth more than several hundred thousand dollars now. He'd sold it for a reportedly outrageous price of $400 an acre and thought he was taking advantage of them.

One of Rudy's sons was Miles "Baby" Ashton. Baby is what everyone called him. He was built like the renowned Rob Roy of Scottish history. He had a barrel chest, overly long arms, a tight small waist and butt. His britches hung on him by imagination. He was a horse of a man. Baby was noted for several things. Firstly, he was as strong as a bull. He could lift more, hold more and was just more powerful than others. Secondly, he could not endure odors or the sight of blood. If a cow came into the pens and was found to have a dead calf inside her, he would leave. He simply could not develop the tolerance to bad odors. Many unpleasant sights and blood, particularly, would set off a reaction. The men all knew this, and took frequent advantage of it. "Hey, Baby, come here. We got us a nasty looking cancer-eye," and Baby would gag predictably. One man in particular, Carlos Falla, pronounced, "Fah-yah", took a fiendish delight in phoning Baby and graphically describing a particularly bad dead-calf delivery. Carlos said he would hear Baby throwing up at the description. But if you were in a tight, there was no finer sight than Baby Ashton, galloping up, uncoiling his rope. The deal was settled at that point. Baby and "Boy" McGown were the first two I ever heard of that rode an ostrich. Baby said, "Tha danged thing could turn on a dime…" Boy spoke up, saying, "Yeah, an' she left you huggin' the fence, didden she?" Boy McGown told us one time, "Boys, I lost 134 pounds last week—my wife moved out to her mama's…"

When it came to cow huntin' and workin' cattle, I don't want to mislead you, you can really get hurt. I have been stomped on, hit, rubbed, mashed, mauled, kicked silly, rolled, cut, hooked, spit and snotted on, along with other similar actions, blunt-horned and head-butted. But the worst I ever got hurt was by a puny little two day-old calf. She couldn't have weighed more than 45 pounds, still wet behind the ears. Her navel had just dried. We had run the calves through the main chute to sort them from their mamas. The little, long-eared whelp kinda' stumbled through, but was soon left behind. All the rank ones had gone on ahead. She walked into the chute, half confused by all the activity. The catch man spooked her but she didn't respond.

It looked like a simple thing to urge her along, so, brazen young lad that I was, I started in to grab her long ears to pull her out. As I leaned over to go into the chute, something spooked her and without warning she bolted forward like a load of buckshot and butted me full throttle in the chin. It was not a killing blow, but it was precise. It probably wouldn't have been so bad if my tongue hadn't been between my right side jaw teeth. (Don't ask how that happened.) I bit the whole right side of my tongue, nearly all the way through. I think all Sonny saw was my wallowing around in front of the chute. I was knocked silly at 4:00 in the afternoon, with no jook joint in sight. Now if that wasn't bad enough, the next few days were sheer misery. I couldn't eat, chew, move my mouth or talk. I managed to get some soup and water down but it hurt like all get out—couldn't even swallow an aspirin...

Sonny didn't comment for a few days and then, in front of several men, remarked, "I been thinkin'. It has been such a pleasure to work with you while you can't talk. I suggested to Daddy that we have all the men bite their tongues so we could get more work and less talkin' done around here. Paw said he didn't think the men would go for it."

I looked at him with sunken haggard eyes, trying to mouth the proper curse words back to him and the laughing audience. It came out as, "Yawl laff, yah krathie hunth-ah-hitheeth." (The pronunciation is best duplicated by holding your tongue with a paper towel or handkerchief while repeating, "Y'all laugh, you crazy sons a..." etc.)

In today's world I could have gotten disability, compensation for pain, suffering and loss of conjugal obligations (if I had been married), unemployment and emotional damages. I just went back to work like the rest of them. None of us knew any better then. Ahh cain't telh y'allh how huch it hurts when yah bhite thruh yher thungh...crust meh, it hreelly hurth...

Becoming a Cowboy at Dark Hammock

"It was rapidly becoming apparent that there was more than meets the eye when it came to these Florida Crackers. I had little trouble in communication and understanding. I had their general common attitude and an appreciation of their humor. I'd suspected the term "Cracker" had a broader meaning. Now I was becoming sure of it."
-HSJ

THERE is a place in Okeechobee County called Dark Hammock, as well as the Ranch so named. I don't know if the Dark Hammock Ranch still exists or is still using the original name; many of them have changed hands over the years, becoming subdivisions. The area was north of us. Yes, true to its name it was a place of dense trees, cabbage palms, tangled vines, and underbrush. A cow, panther, or bear could slip in there and disappear. Hubert coined a phrase about clever cows or bulls giving us the vanishing act, saying, "They can slip through there like a dose of salts in a widow woman…" (I failed to see the appropriateness of the comment but had a good idea what he meant.)

If it weren't for the cow dogs, finding the cattle would have been near impossible. Somehow, I guess by experience and cow sense, the men knew where the cattle would come out of the thick woods. You could set your horse, listening in the cool of the mornings, and follow the progress of the ones whose job it was to "bring-im." It was not easy to stay on your horse in these somewhat impenetrable areas. The limbs and vines made it difficult to follow, even on foot, whereas the cattle could lower their heads, wedging their way in. Even a tenacious puppy or sorry cur dog was useful in cleaning cattle out of the dense hammocks.

When we finished our work, it was time for our crew to move over to Dark Hammock. It was about 6-8 miles as the proverbial crow flies. We could cut through the corner of the ranch, going almost directly to their main cow pens. I guess we could have taken a trailer full of horses over but I am so thankful we didn't, for that first summer I would have missed the rides of a lifetime. My best memories are of those pre-dawn mornings, riding through the woods heading to Dark Hammock Ranch. I recollect these trips vividly. We'd be ready about 4:30 to 5:00, saddled in the poor light of the barn way before daylight. (I never understood why the lights in the horse barn were so dim. It could have been the years of accumulated fly specks and dust that covered them.)

Thunder was a little rough the first thing in the mornings; it took several miles for us to settle in together. I recall riding behind Hubert when he would light up a Camel; the smoke would dissipate in the still morning air as I rode into it. I never smell Camel cigarette smoke that I don't think of those times. Riding through the brush, our boots and pants legs would become wet with dew from the palmettos and myrtle bushes. Our stirrups would push aside the palm fans. They rustled as they sprang back. These noises marked our passing through thick brushy places, zigzagging through openings or following barely discernible cow or game trails. We kept track of those who were behind us by these slaps and rattles. We spooked deer, armadillos, raccoons, and all kinds of birds on their way to work, so to speak. The startled deer ran out a ways from us, turned and stopped to see if we followed or were indeed a threat to them. Then they would turn back, flag their white tails straight up, and prance-jog stiffly away. Some quietly slipped off among the pines and palmettos, not in much of a hurry at all. These morning trips, though not numerous, were a satisfying change in the routine. I looked forward to them, saddle tender though I was. I was young, lean and ready and like all youngsters, figured I'd live forever.

Didn't George Bernard Shaw say that youth is wasted on the young?

It was at Dark Hammock that I began to think that I might really have a chance to earn the respect of those Cracker cowboys. I tried everything I knew to help. My enthusiasm usually made up for my lack of ability. I watched and learned. The crossbred cows were rank, the Brahma bulls, ranker. Sonny and Ephraim said that I was better in the pens than on horseback. I just tried to do what they told me and, also I liked working the pens more. To illustrate the point, Ephraim gave me a bad cussing at Dark Hammock one time when I got in his way as he was trying to separate a cow and her calf on Peanut. The activity was out in an open pasture. We had moved the cattle alongside a fence, holding them only with men on horseback, a couple of cow dogs and a considerable amount of strength of will. Peanut was being a little uncooperative, too. Every time he had the cow going in the right way, she'd spot me and bolt back. I just didn't move out of the way fast enough. To this day I don't know who was the dumber, me or Thunder. That was the first cussing I had had in a while so, like a stomped on cur dog, I slinked back to the back, letting someone else have my spot in the circle. He later made light of it, kidding me a little, recognizing that it was my inexperience and not laziness.

On the Day I Became a Cowboy we were at Dark Hammock Ranch. We had almost finished and had separated the cows from the big weanling calves, destined for sale as steers or for herd replacements as breeder heifers. I was in the back, closing gates. I had just taken up my position there when I heard a lot of hollering, "Stop 'er, catch 'er. She jumped the fence and is headin' for the cows!" I climbed up on the fence and saw immediately what the ruckus was all about: a big heifer coming my way, zigzagging through all the open gates, headed for the gap at my end of the pens. I knew that if she got past me, she'd be home free for a reunion with her mama. I didn't have time to do anything but get in the center of the gate opening. Here she came with a head of steam. I sidestepped her snort and head-butt and fell in on her neck. It must have looked like I was trying my hand at steer wrestling, but there were no horns to grab. The weight differential was notable. I was a blistering 145 pounds, like a night crawler with his guts slung out, and she was a whopping 450 pounds. She bucked, kicked, snorted and scrubbed me along the fence, trying to shake me off. I knew I had gotten kicked a few times, but didn't feel a thing until the next morning. I held on tighter than the bark on a tree. I had the proverbial "tiger by the tail," only she was a heifer! She dragged me it felt like all over that place and I was never so glad to see a crew of men coming toward me. I needed relief and I needed it fast. I had slowed her down apparently enough for them to reach us and finally capture the furious animal.

Struggling up with my shirt in rags and kick marks all over my jeans, for some reason I reached for my handkerchief. I guess it was to wipe the manure out of my eyes, but I found that my pocket was packed with cow manure. In fact, all my pockets were packed with cow manure, as were my boots. It doesn't take much cow manure to say "all my pockets were packed"…Well, the laughter erupted into whoops. They even called for the other men to come see me. One said, "Boys, I wish you'd look at that…" I never will understand why tore off shirts, splinters, skinned knuckles, back pockets and boots full of manure increases one's status among cowboys.

Mama didn't see the honor nor the humor in it. It was the first time she wouldn't let me in the house. As I recall, I went out to the swimming pool, shucked off most of my clothes and dove in. At least I could approach the house for a towel after that.

On the long rides home from Dark Hammock we all were caught in the moment of fatigue and satisfaction that the job that day had been well done. Half asleep in the saddle, but listening, I picked up many little bits of knowledge about place names. For instance, there was a place the old timers called "Dead (politically incorrect term deleted) Bay". The story was that a Negro man was found deceased there barefooted and clad only in bib overalls. It was a mystery where he came from or where he was going. There was "Jugueass Slough", appropriately named for the man who backed into a meat cooking stick during a dinner break. I don't know how to spell, "jugue" or "jewgue". It rhymes with, "fugue" and is synonymous with "poke, jab, nudge or prod". Crackers sometimes used this term in the context of diverting away, veering off or making a getaway.

North and west of the ranch was Panther Ford, named for obvious reasons. There were landmarks like Lone Pine, Double Gates, Opal, Bull Hole, the Evans Place, the Raulerson Grove, the Oak Field, Walkups Island, Duck Pond, Dark Hammock, the Dynamite Ditch, Gator Hole, Why-tha-hell Pens, Bear Wallow, Hen Scratch Ranch, Last Chance Cattle Company and the like. The "Why-tha-hell Pens" were named because the cow pens were built close to a massive oak, but just outside the shaded area in full sun. It was as if the original builder was being sadistic to all who would work there. Not only was there no shade, but also they were tucked in a place sheltered from prevailing winds. The poor souls who worked there did so in the full sun all day where there was little or no air movement. No breeze could work its way into the void. Every time I showed up to work there, someone would comment, "Why-tha-hell did they build these cow pens here?" The name stuck.

The land looks different after dark. Out on the prairie, you could keep to a general direction, go in a straight line, using the outlines of lone dead pines, old roadbeds or trails as landmarks, or stars. In the deep woods, you could get disoriented. Fences came in handy when you were lost. Follow one long enough and you'd find a place you recognized. Me and Thunder sure were both glad to see the barn those dark nights.

One of the conversations I vividly recall was on one ride to the barn when we had to take some cattle through a cabbage hammock next to the first grove. We were having difficulty in keeping them tightly bunched together, afraid they would get away from us and scatter into a big pasture.

We then would have to start all over. There was an air of excitement as we plunged into the thick of the hammock. We all got separated some; we were on our own at that point. Finally, I could hear the popping of the dried cabbage palm boots and the swooshing of the underbrush as they came right at me. I took off at a run trying to head them off. Apparently, I had not tightened my cinch very well because the saddle started going sideways. I fell butt over tea kettle, as they say, right in front of Sonny who was blazing new trails in the hammock. He rode by grinning at me as I recovered the reins and started to reset and cinch the saddle. After the excitement had leveled off, we had the furry beasts under control. On the way home Sonny turned to one of the men, loudly asking,

"What do you think of a fella who stops to take a nap when your cattle are making a getaway?" Course, I sheepishly tried to explain. He replied, "Maybe you ought to stay home at night and get more sleep before comin' to work..." We all laughed. I thought of Jack Page falling off his horse.

We headed home. Boy! Once again, I liked the sound of that... home...

Hiard, If Ya Want To, Sit on That Post And Run the Dipping Vat Gate

"I'm not so sure it's good to think back to my childhood memories, because I end up feeling happy and sad at the same time, and that gives me a weird 'neutral' feeling…"
Jack Handley, in *Deep Thoughts*

MY first sure-enough-by-myself assignment in the pens, after learning how not to get cow caught or to stand in the way of running men and cattle, was manning the gate exiting the dip-vat pen. I sat on a big corner-post, opening and closing the gate where the freshly dipped cattle climbed out. There they stood for a few minutes, dripping the excess dip that flowed back into the vat. As jobs went it was what is called a no-brainer; however, it was perfect for a fella of limited experience, involved but out of the way, doing an essential if somewhat boring task.

Don't tell anybody you have a dipping vat on your property; they'll test all the wells for arsenic residues all around the place. Testing is a good idea, but a minute trace of arsenic is not necessarily a bad thing. For example, during the Crusades, around 1060 AD, there are tales about Spanish women who daily drank tiny amounts of arsenic. The Crusader knights courted these women, causing no small amount of ridicule among the Spaniards because some of these women were well over sixty years old. These beautiful women had taken the arsenic to keep their skin smooth. It worked, too. It was later named, "Fowler's Solution." I don't think I would recommend it. I've wondered if that's the reason so many Cracker women are so pretty, from drinking trace amounts of arsenic from wells near old dipping vats.

So there I would sit on my corner post, pushing the exit gate open for those cattle that made the jump-dive into the long deep vat. It's a wonder we didn't drown them all, but they were hearty and took it in stride. It was a monotonous job that had brief dramatic episodes when a bull would bow up at the hordes of men and dogs. My seat was the best in the house when any bull had enough of this foolishness. I recall one episode where two bulls got into a fight directly below me and demolished all the fencing around me. I was like a shikepoke, sitting on a bare single post amidst a raging bullfight. A shikepoke is a common name for a small, skinny pond heron that perches on posts in creeks and ponds hunting for minnows and frogs. According to Hubert, the name was quite fitting for my predicament.

I thought about diving into the dip vat, but that was the last resort. Hubert was strangely amused as he watched me frantically search for someplace to climb. I suppose I was a never-ending source of entertainment for him.

After being graduated from gate man on the dipping vat, I was assigned the task of poking the cows down the alleyway. The classic noise required for this job was a loud "smooching" sound. But any sound or word would work, like, "Hah!" or "Heh!" Anything worked that startled them into moving along.

Paw was right when he said, "Some bulls only get upset when they are separated and isolated. Turn in some cows for company...they will usually settle down. Every now and then you'll get an outlaw bull or cow. They are really mean and will look you up in the pens." We liked to sell the outlaws.

When he told me that Brahmas were predictable, that they will be led but will not be driven, he paused, glanced my way with his little half-smile and said, "Kinda like your mama..." He advised me to look for a leader cow or bull get that one headed in the right direction and the others would follow. I learned from him also to watch what happens when a threat comes to the herd. The bulls will come to the edge, the cows behind them and the calves sheltered in the middle. He was a student of the breed and the species, in general.

The best cowmen make the cattle think something you wanted them to do was their idea. I have no scientific basis for this assessment. I do know that a horse will respond to that training method. More than once, Sonny and Hubert blocked an open gate to settle them. We'd just sit there a while and talk, let the mamas find their babies. Finally, one or two cows would "discover" that the man in the gate had moved, leaving the gate open. A few would tentatively start through and others would follow. Sometimes they would all try to go at once, as if they thought they were executing a break away from us. I can hear the squeaking fence staples even today in my mind. One of us would ride up close to the gate, somewhat slowing the escape. But once they all took off, it was hard to control the mad dash under mob panic.

When an otherwise wild cow reverts to a non-aggressive state at calving it is an amazing thing. Cowboys throughout time have helped many a cow deliver at the end of lariats in hammocks and even open pastures without much fear of being cow-caught. But it was, "Lord help me!" when she was through the delivery. She'd revert back into a wild thing once that baby was out and she'd eat your sack lunch over it. Your immediate post-delivery problem was getting the ropes off her. Many times, we'd leave one man holding the tail of the downed cow. The tail was passed between her back legs and the man would take a hold, putting his weight on her back end. Cows get up by raising the rear end first; the extra weight on her pelvis gave the holder leverage and prevented her rising. Once everyone was mounted, ropes removed, the holder would release the tail and high-ball it toward his horse while a mounted cowboy would distract the half-crazed cow. I've read that females don't know when to quit when it comes to defending the baby. And I've observed something like this in working these cattle. The bulls will fight until one backs away, then it's over. But a cow fighting over her baby is not inclined to quit. As a cowboy might put it, "She reminds me of my first wife..." As man domesticates animals much of this natural wildness is diluted. In the Brahmas of the sixties and seventies there was still some strong instinctive behavior.

Boy, You Thought About Goin' to College?

AFTER that first hard but satisfying three months, I "decided" to try to go to college. The reason I emphasize "decided" is because I now realize that Paw worked things so that I would think it was my idea. I'm sure he planned some of the real-world work to teach me that there might be a better way to make a living. The real reason may lie somewhere between the hard work on the ranch, which Paw had probably devised, and that military service somewhere in the world had become a likelihood. One way or another, college looked like a good opportunity, especially after a few months in the blazing Florida sun in the cow pens, hoeing and hand-fertilizing orange trees or banging around in pastures in the Jeep planting grass seed. Though I liked those things I was inclined to better myself. No one in my first family had ever been to college. In the back of my mind, maybe that was the reason to attend. After all had he not said they would help me? Was I overstepping my place? Why would such a man take the time to encourage me? I knew he loved my mother, and I strongly sensed that he also loved me. Or was I seeing things through rose colored glasses? Nevertheless, in the shadow of his encouragement I stepped out into this unknown territory.

Paw and Sonny had gone to the University of Florida, so that was my logical choice. He said that he had set aside some bonds for the kids to attend college. He would give me a bond and, when cashed, it would be enough for a year. I was a little unsure about all this, thinking, after all, I hadn't done anything to deserve it. Apparently, he didn't see it that way. Here was unconditional support I'd never known.

As if the time table were being controlled by an unknown Hand, I was late in applying for that fall's college enrollment. What would I do in the meantime until I could get accepted? It was the best possible thing that could have happened to me. While Paw was sitting in the office late one summer afternoon, I asked him if it would be okay if I continued working full time on the ranch. I was a little apprehensive about it, thinking, "I ain't much count yet…but maybe they would find a spot for me…" But surprise, he agreed it would be a good idea. Though I initially thought it a disastrous event at the time, Paw said, "Who cares. If you go at 18 or 25, it doesn't make any difference in the big picture of things." He was right.

It was a time for more growth, for experience, for wisdom, for enlarging of boundaries that I would never have attempted otherwise. Entering college then would have denied me a year of wonderful experiences. It would have hampered my development. Unbeknownst to me at the time, this was the moment when I think he decided to expand my boundaries in hard work. Was there a method to his madness? I hit the ground running with a glimpse of expanding self-confidence and quite a bit of ignorant enthusiasm—still a bit of a puppy I'm afraid…

So You Want to Work on a Ranch, Huh?

"I am an old man now and have known many troubles, but most of them never happened."
-Mark Twain

IF the horse barn was the beginning of all cow-working activities, the machine shop was the same for all other ranch work. "The shop", brings back memories of men talking, dogs fighting, re-fueling tractors and loading equipment, wire, seed, feed and fertilizer. Everything started there and you could catch a ride there to your job. It was also a good meeting place for about any activity. "Meet me at the shop…" was a common request. Saturday noon paydays occurred there as well as its being a gathering place before and after hunting when dressing out deer carcasses. There was a tradition of cutting off a deer hunter's shirttails if he'd missed an easy shot. This was done as a cooperative effort. Two or three would hold you down, while someone did the cutting. It was like a fraternity initiation but involved a sharp knife. One's hind end shrunk a little when the knife came close…But usually everyone just stood around talking, reliving the hunt.

The shop smelled of motor oil, paint, grass seed, diesel, creosote, and citrus fertilizer. I don't know why, but one day Hubert decided to slip up behind me and give me a rank bear hug. He slid his arms under mine and proceeded to squeeze my chest like a boa constrictor, laughing that low laugh he had. I only weighed about 150 pounds at the time, compared to his good solid 240, but after a considerable amount of hard work, I had become leaner, harder and what they called, "skinny tough". Reaching up and grabbing his head, I sent his hat flying off. I slipped my leg inside his, pulling his off the ground. We fell in a heap on the concrete floor, all 400 pounds of us. He let go just in time for me to get my breath. Laughing while he rolled up, he was ready for another round. I left for the safety of the nearest tractor. One trick had worked. Why press your luck? I don't know exactly what was said. I was busy at the time. I expect if Paw had been there, he'd have grumbled, "Y'all are worse than a bunch of (*expletive for doomed deleted*) cur dog puppies." I tell you now Hubert loved me. A cracked rib was his way of showing it.

The early morning meetings at the shop where we all gathered for assignments became little soap operas and gossip fests. We'd hear about who got hurt, how it happened, what and how equipment was torn up, who needed to go get parts and what the plan was for the day.

My horizons expanded in my first adventure as a sure-enough full-time ranch hand. I had worked enough to see that I liked it. When not working, I would wander around the ranch by myself with the dogs. We'd all run armadillos or tree coons in the orange groves. It was great fun. The dogs were on ready all the time. When I asked if I could continue working until college acceptance, Paw said he would pay me $10 a day for a five and a half day week (that's about $70-80 per day in today's money.)

I figured my first assignment would be with one of the grove crews, but found that he had something special for me—a total change of direction. He met me at the shop with four cases of bright aluminum-gray Rust-oleum paint. We loaded two gallons and related supplies into the Jeep. He took me to an artesian well capped off with a huge wellhead valve, reminding me of the kind you see on heavy duty water valves or oil wells. You had to crank open the valve with both hands. The whole thing was massive. These were artesian wells fed from the subterranean aquifer used for irrigating the groves and pastures. Some of these wells would spit up fossilized shark's teeth and shells, a sign of Florida's prehistoric history.

The whole thing was covered in rank grass. Under it fire ants had set up camp. He showed me how to hoe back all the weeds, dig down below the earth level at the base of the pipe, and clean off all the rust with a stiff wire brush. With no other tool or mechanical assistance, it was all done by wire brush, muscle and determination. He then demonstrated how to apply the rust inhibitor paint to the whole wellhead.

So I set about cleaning and preparing the well for painting. He left me, showing up in the Jeep several hours later. We loaded the remaining paint in the green Jeep and went home. The next day, they gave me a truck. I went alone from then on, taking some lunch and a water jug. Did you know there were about twelve wells on the place? I painted every blamed one of them; even so I was plum proud of the accomplishment. Paw never said a word about it other than, "How you doin', buddy?" when he'd come by to pick me up on those days I went home for dinner.

Everyone thinks it is so cool being a ranch hand. They forget about the oppressive heat, rashes, violent rain storms, cold, lightning, skint fingers, scraped knees, soggy boots, snakes, fire ants, mosquitoes, wasps, sunburn, sand gnats, spiders and boredom. But he knew patience was what I needed and he was determined I'd learn it.

Was he up to something?

Donna Reminds Me of an Ol' Gal I Usta Know

"Martha remembers a time long ago when the only warning of hurricanes, other than natural portents plain to the wise, was the whistle of the train four miles away at the village. In the hurricane season the engineer gave an agreed signal in announcement, and in winter another to tell of an impending freeze."
-Marjorie Kinnan Rawlings, in *Cross Creek*

THOUGH as a general rule we knew what we would be doing for the next week or two, at times there would be radical interruptions in the plans due to impending weather or some other crisis. At the machine shop, one morning in September 1960, there was a subtle change in the atmosphere. Sonny and Paw were considerably more serious than usual. A hurricane was brewing off the coasts of the Caribbean Islands. They had named her "Donna." Paw said the reason they named them after women is because they could change their minds at any time about where they were going. Of course, this was before political correctness became fashionable. This was all new to me. I had no idea what was to happen.

We gathered as usual but with an added air of anticipation. Paw and Sonny gave directives in a suggestive form usually unfamiliar to most employees. They'd say things like, "Well, if y'all want to, we need to clear the cows and calves out the big marsh pasture. Leave the east side gates open to the hammocks, so they can go in there for protection." Many times I heard them preface directives with, "If you want to." This was a signal that if you had a better idea, they were listening. One would say something like, "We sure need to have the tractors moved to the Double Gates barn." Some of the men, Hubert in particular, would ask questions, give a good method for accomplishing the task or make comments. It surely was a nice atmosphere for the men. They didn't mind at all. We all easily got on the same page, even if the task was hard. Sometimes the directives didn't make a lot of sense to the men. In scientific jargon, there was an "insufficiency of data". We just couldn't see the big picture. I think we all appreciated the fact that we were only responsible for our assigned jobs, although that didn't exclude us from doing what was in the best interest of the ranch. Most of us instinctively knew there were times to leave our assignments and to step out and take care of business. When you saw a broken fence line or a gate that was torn up, you took care of it. When you suspected an odd sound in a tractor, you shut down and got help. You pulled a fellow worker out of a bog when necessary. You never left a cornered or injured man without support in the cow pens, going to him to distract the beast that was upon him or to drag him out while others took the brunt of the bull's aggression. We did it willingly, letting the ultimate responsibility ride with the men who directed us, but ready to help anywhere we could. There was a team spirit, a camaraderie, a kinship…There was quiet security in that.

A couple of days before Hurricane Donna came to town we were told that we had to clear the cattle out of the big marsh—if we wanted to. The men were told to get things put up, battened down and ready. They were told to go home and prepare for the storm when they'd finished. Groceries had to be bought; candles and other supplies were needed. I remember the clouds were taking odd formations, all flowing from the southeast. They looked like orange ridges of buttermilk, sweeping toward the Avon Park Bombing Range, Ft Meade, and Brooksville. We saddled up and headed for the marsh. The cattle were troubled, milling in loose groups that was not normal. They knew instinctively something was up. The winds were beginning to intensify.

Little rain storms hit, sheets of it dissipating just as quickly as they came on us. I thought I could hear a low moan in the distance, like a far-away night train roaring down some track during a downpour. It was a vibrating hum that was slowly but steadily growing louder. Palm fans and small branches were sailing past us in winds that sounded like great waves of running waters. Leaves slipped by as a blur. The rain began to fly in swishing curtains and sheets at odd diagonal angles, followed by a relatively short calm. But off in the distance one could hear a distinct mounting roar from the increasing winds, one you never forget. Out over the distant woods the trees undulated like ocean waves as the gusts moved through their tops. Occasionally there was a crash or crack as some weak tree broke or fell. Even massive oaks toppled over, twisting up obscene broad flat plates of matted roots. Cabbage palms fell with loud thuds, taking branches of surrounding trees with them. Ponds had leaf strewn ripples and little white caps, canals looked like black-gray chenille bed spreads. It was awesome, terrifying, beautiful, memorable…

The cattle gathered with little difficulty. We headed them toward the camp house hammocks, the direction they were inclined to go. Thunder was a little uptight, a little too responsive. It was difficult to hold him still while others sidled the cattle toward the fence. As we approached the hammocks, Sonny gave me the go-ahead sign to open the gates and get out of the way of the herd. I remember riding as hard as I could for the gate, hat pulled down tight, huge raindrops pelting my face and stinging fiercely. Jumping off Thunder, rain water pouring off the front of my hat, I fumbled with the chain hook that acted as a gate lock. I could hear the rumble of nervous cattle coming my way. As I opened the gate, it swung freely out of the way, exposing an escape to the hammocks, a refuge in a wild sea of activity. The cattle moved into the hammock orderly. Several cows went through, stopped just past the fence, turned and bawled for their babies. Once reunited, they led off into the thick woods.

We gathered in a tight wad, riding with our hats tilted downward, backs to the rain when we could, slickers and skin soaked through. After a very, very long ride to the horse barn, we unsaddled the horses and turned them out. Rain blew into some stalls, though the majority of them were dry. The barn's tin roof cracked and popped and leaves and twigs blew into the alley way. Acorns hit and rattle-hopped downward on the tin. The chickens had disappeared to no one knew where. The dogs got into and under things, laying heads on paws or directly on the dirt of the barn floor. They rolled their eyes at you when you approached them, but not make any effort to leave their hidey holes. They weren't particularly interested in socializing. We all went home to dry out. My boots were so wet and socks so sodden, I could remove them only with difficulty. After dry clothes, a cup of coffee was real contentment. I sat by the window, watching the fury. It was to be a two-day ordeal. The cabbage palms began to bend to horizontal in the winds with their fans flattened into curved willowy paintbrushes.

The day before the storm hit, Paw and I had ridden the Jeep out to inspect the groves, all heavy in early fruit. It represented a year's work. There was a considerable sum of money hanging on the trees. He didn't say a word as we drove from grove to grove. Finally, as was his pattern, he visibly relaxed and said, almost unconsciously, his usual, "Uh-huh." Now he looked out at the trees already thrashing from early gusts and murmured, apparently to the wildly bobbing fruit, "Hold on boys, the winds a-comin'." Far as I know he slept like a baby that night.

During the hurricane Sonny came over with a wind gauge he'd gotten somewhere for the airplane hangar. He'd already flown his J-3 Cub to a safe airport in Avon Park. Well, we decided to go out and test the wind speed. I remember trying to stand up with this whirling thing in my hands. I'd hold it, both of us staggering against the mounting wind and he'd read it, giving a little summary, "Thirty, thirty-five...thirty-seven..." I didn't understand why we couldn't easily stand in thirty mile per hour winds. We concluded that we were underestimating the wind speed; the gauge had to be mounted on something stationary to be accurate.

Sonny was concerned about flooding. Citrus can take rising or falling water for some limited time, but standing water will kill the roots. We had one particular new grove that had a pump in place but no engine to drive it. With a flash of insight, I asked, "Does it hurt a diesel tractor to run in the open?" "No," he replied. "Well, why don't we drive a tractor over, hook up the power-take-off and let 'er run during the storm?" He agreed. We did this and the thing purred on for three or four days, dumping thousands of gallons of water out of the grove. It was odd to go out there and hear the steady droning of the diesel while the rest of the world blew and bucked and whipped chaotically.

Conditions at the house worsened as the wind changed its angle of attack. Water blew in under the back doors and I spent a considerable amount of time sopping up and wringing out the towels. The water surely did a number on the ranch that year, but the effects of Donna were over almost as fast as they came on us. We made a trip out the next morning in the post-hurricane heat and humidity, finding the old railroad grade that ran through the ranch flooded and washed out near the Double Gates. I was amazed that it was hard to stand in as little as six to eight inches of rushing water. After a round on the ranch, we knew there was work to be done after Ol' Donna. There were wash-outs to fill, trees to remove from fences, gates to repair and groves to check. A few citrus trees had split limbs. They had to be removed or, if not seriously damaged, pruned. The grove pumps ran a few more days to remove excessive water to keep the trees from stress and root-drowning. The water control structures located at some key points in the drainage canals were opened, turning millions of gallons of black water to Taylor Creek and ultimately to Lake Okeechobee. The excess water would seek its way through the lake to the various canals leading to the east coast, to the south through the Everglades or west out the Caloosahatchee River toward the Gulf. Slowly and steadily the water levels dropped until the marsh pasture fences could be seen.

Alligators moved around, looking for good sites to set up housekeeping. The water fowl loved these conditions, locating good points where water narrowed into rivulets, funneling minnows to ambush sites. Fast moving water ran through the pasture culverts, washing out some of them deep enough to stand upright in. The bream, bass, gars and others sought the swirling, fast-running waters coming from the culverts. They'd gather *en masse* to attack the hapless mosquito larvae, tadpoles and minnows.

Things settled down in a few days. The cattle quietly returned to their routines, emerging from the hammocks at early day, grazing out into the soggy, but lush marsh pastures, resting in shade during the hottest part of the day and returning to the shelter of the hammocks at evening. The owls, raccoons, armadillos, insects, birds and other varmints went back to work. The night shift was particularly busy with all the new insects out and about.

There was evidence of the storm all over the yard at home. It took Purty Jesse several days to gather up and haul off the debris and cabbage fans. Most hammocks just looked a little disheveled. Paw said hurricanes were nature's haircuts.

Grove work

NOW, I knew which side of a horse to mount, when to run from cattle and how to not be trampled by others, how to paint artesian wells, and how to work hard. I had learned basic skills that would serve me well in the future. Next they introduced me to citrus grove care.

This endeavor had many aspects, among which were grove design and construction, tree selection and planting, fertilizing, watering, and spraying for parasites and diseases. I was introduced to the exercise of tree planting and applying fertilizer by hand. When fertilizing we were issued five-gallon buckets. We took potato sacks and made a crude strap that attached to the bucket handle with coarse wire. You put your head through the strap and let the combined weight of the granulated fertilizer and the bucket rest on the neck and shoulders. With the strap held up and open, you could insert your head, rest the strap on the left side of your neck and have your right hand free to apply the granules. The filled bucket weighed about thirty-five pounds. I vividly remember that a day of this activity left me with a sore neck, back, arms and elbows. The trick was to get a handful of the fertilizer as you approached the tree, then throw the granules out in a smooth motion that applied it in an even spread. You'd get in a walking rhythm, spreading the granules and moving on to tree after tree, all day long.

Little trees usually took one good heaping handful. Bigger trees took much more; you'd have to walk around the tree and apply several handfuls. The object was an even spread near the tree line, the edge of the branches. The work was tedious and the strains of "Ol' Man River" and "Nobody Knows the Trouble I've Seen" come to mind when I think of it. My shoulder would get so sore that you couldn't touch it with a powder puff. Day after day this continued.

Sleeping at noon on sacks of fertilizer in the little barn near the groves, with radiated heat on our faces from the tin roof was a mixed blessing. Rain breaks were wonderful. We slept, whittled, made toothpicks, drank water and talked. Those violent thunderstorms were awesome to watch. Just before they would hit, if we were in the sun, we'd experience an intense humidity and heat. If the wind picked up and clouds started covering us, we could usually smell the rain or see a gray curtain of rain coming at us. We'd head for the trucks or barns at the first droplets hit us.

My hands got rough and calloused. I wore gloves when I could. Cuts burned something fierce. This went on and on, like the clover seeding (which I'll tell you about later.). One thing was clear; however, I knew I had done a day's work when we were through. I eventually changed to different clothing. I used to wear lightweight short-sleeved shirts, but ended up in heavy long-sleeved denim shirts. They afforded protection from the sun, chemicals and insects. I could also wet them down and they would stay cooler. Just the opposite from today's thought, I had little skin exposed while wearing gloves, long sleeved shirts, buttoned down, a hat, jeans and boots. I found this helpful to a blue-eyed, blond-headed Welshman. Too bad I didn't think about preventing hearing damage until it was too late.

We modernized up to a fertilizer spreader, a red one. It was a squared tank-like affair that was pulled and powered by a tractor. It had aircraft tires. There was a platform at the end where a worker could stand and shut it on and off. It had the means of channeling the granules to one side. As I recall, we didn't fertilize the grounds between small trees, that would waste product. But big tree rows were continuously fed fertilizer, shutting down only at the ends of rows at the turn-around. In the pastures, we ran it continuously. We had bulk fertilizer delivered in big hoppers that allowed easier filling of the spreader. It was still hot, sweaty work, with plenty of sunburn and mosquito bites, but my arms and shoulders worked better after a day on it. The high throttle rates, the sound of raw power, the knowledge that I was doing some good was pleasant to me. I couldn't allow rain to get into the spreader as this set up a tremendous corrosion problem. Even dew was a hazard. We usually parked only in the barns at the end of the day. When through with the fertilizing, we had to wash out all fertilizer and spray the beast down with kerosene to prevent rusting.

Another monster machine I enjoyed was the orange-colored sprayer, also pulled by a powerful tractor. It probably held 500 gallons of water or mixed emulsified oils. We had to apply oils for the citrus mite infestations. It was used for spraying pastures with only one man driving and controlling the spray. In the groves it took two men to run it, one driving and one controlling the spray at the back. On little trees, the spray man shut the spray on and off as each tree was passed. The spray rack had several adjustable nozzles on a swivel that could be aimed at the little trees as you approached them at about 3 miles per hour, turn on the spray, cover the tree with spray, then shut off the nozzles. Here again, a few trees were no problem, but a whole grove of 500 or more got old after several non-stop hours. It was rewarding, however.

We'd have to stop spraying, mark our last tree, refill the tank from overhead pipes and mix in the additives. This operation took some time and I'd walk around or sit under the sprayer to rest. Once loaded, we'd head back to our stopping point. In the big groves, we'd set spray nozzles to blast up and out on both sides of the rig and one man could drive through the groves and hit two rows at once. As he came to the end of the row, he'd just spray with one side of the nozzles, opening up both sides once he got back in among the rows. I can still smell the spray today. It was hot down in among the big trees. We watched for rain, since the application had to have a little drying time. Many an hour was spent on that rig. I sprayed pastures for weeds, too. We'd used "2,4,D", a weed killer that didn't hurt grass.

I remember bogging the thing down in a few places. It weighed 2 tons when fully loaded, not counting the weight of the tractor and the sprayer. I'd have to walk in, find somebody to take me to another tractor, put up with all sorts of colorful comments and go pull 'er out. Word got around. Paw would ask at the dinner table, "Boy, did you find any bogs today?" "Yeah, over near Boggy Branch", I said, looking down at my dinner plate.

He grinned, "I swear, if there's one bog on this place you will find it." Oddly, when he said it there was no trace of derision, criticism, anger or frustration. It was almost comforting. He was saying, "Lighten up on yourself, boy."

I ran a retractable tiller. This was a device attached to the side of a powerful tractor. It had hydraulic connections, so that when properly set up, it allowed a driver to drive beside the trees and till the sandy soil to powder, grinding up weeds, shrubs and bushes at the same time. As I got close to a tree trunk, I could pull a lever and the fast rotating blades would retract out of the way. When I passed the tree trunk, I could reverse the lever to put the tiller back in line. Two passes per row, on either side of the trees, resulted in a wide tilled swath of powdered, weed-free soil. This machine required much concentration. I had to watch the angle of the tractor, the speed, the RPM's of the tiller and tractor, the depth of the tiller and the proximity of the tiller to the tree. If I didn't concentrate, I could bark a tree or destroy it entirely. I enjoyed this machine but it didn't allow much fooling around—which I was want to do on occasion. I'd get so fixated that my back and neck would stiffen up. But, boy, it was a wonder since hand-hoeing was a real job.

It surely didn't take long for me to get to liking the thing. I remember skinning a re-set tree. I told Paw. He asked what happened. I told him I lost my concentration for a bit.

He said, "You owe me $3.50," and grinned. I never paid him, but I noticed that I was in on the re-setting of trees in that grove not long afterwards.

One winter night Paw, Mama and I were listening to the Citrus Mutual forecasts on the radio. They predicted severe frost and freeze warnings for our area. Mature citrus fruit could withstand cold for very short lengths of time. A rule of thumb has been 28 degrees for four hours and 26 for two hours. Little trees were more susceptible to freezing; the leaves would look like they'd been burnt by fire. If they got so cold that the bark split, it was all over. Some tried to thwart the freezes by mounding sand over the trunks of the little trees. This would protect the trunk though the top portion may be lost. In that event the trunks would later re-sprout new growth. Ambient humidity and the amount of water in the trees had a bearing on cold damage, too. If trees were in very good condition the grove would survive as low as 15 degrees though the foliage and fruit was lost. When the fruit froze it was ruined. It took a while for the fruit to fall off and rot. Many caretakers would go to the groves early after a severe freeze, cutting test fruit here and there to see if it contained ice crystals.

Paw told me that as early as the thirties the California type metal smudge pots were used to keep trees within the critical temperatures. These were oil burners with four foot tall chimneys that radiated heat. When needed they were set out throughout groves. The rest of the time they rusted in storage for a year or two. People would sit up all night trying to time the lighting of the oil. Many children spent sleepless nights keeping these pots going. A sack full of money could be spent on oil every night that the groves needed firing. The warnings of impending freezes were given the afternoons before and grove owners were alert for these bulletins. In our area smudge pots were not used as much as in the more northerly locations like Hardee, Highlands and Polk Counties, and even farther north. You could smell the fumes for miles. Most of the groves that were planted up west of Orlando are gone now. In the sixties they claimed at the Citrus Tower near Haines City that one could see one million citrus trees from the top of it. Three back-to-back severe freezes in the early nineties wiped them out. I expect the grove owners came to the same conclusion as the Alabama farmer who expressed his conclusions on replanting a crop, "Bubba, you can make a whole lot more money off'n an acre of house trailers than you can on one of cotton."

Years ago when the citrus groves were threatened by a freeze, the old timers would set fatwood pine fires. Piles of literd wood were strategically placed near the edges of groves for quick access. The old timers said that there's nothing more beautiful than a grove shining in the orange-colored light of literd fires. Some people were very particular in site selection for planting their groves. Groves adjacent to large lakes fared better due to re-tained heat. There were places called cold pockets where it was a waste of time to plant citrus. Paw said that cold air traveled like dense cold water, flowing down invisible paths, settling in the lowest area. When the tempera-ture dropped these pockets were the first to freeze. Some growers kept re-planting them. The trees would do fine for a few years, only to refreeze.

We were set up differently. The groves were planted on a "bed and ditch" design. Between every other row of trees was a waist-deep ditch the length of the grove; on alternate rows was a 10" deep furrow with sloping sides. This allowed water to flow from the well heads into the shallow furrow and seep out to the tree roots while the deeper ditch allowed excess water to flow out to the drainage ditches at the ends of the rows.

Another advantage was the ability to run water into the groves when a freeze was expected. The flowing artesian water steamed in the cold though it was only some 20-30 degrees higher than the ambient winter air tempera-ture. It warmed the grove somewhat and was very labor efficient. If we knew a freeze was coming, we'd ride all the groves, turning water into the beds.

I would sometimes go out in the night with Paw or Sonny to appraise the threat. We didn't have to do much because all the preparations had been made during the day, but we just wanted to feel the danger to the trees. Two o'clock in the morning to daybreak was a critical period. If it was still quiet, the stars shining like diamonds on black velvet, we knew the cold could be serious. Clouds and windy conditions were more likely to prevent damage by holding the temperature at tolerable levels. Marjorie Kinnan Rawlings wrote, "The air is so still that voices from far away sound very close at hand...

It is too cold for the birds to sing an evensong and they go to bed early and uneasily. The first stars are visible while the west is still rosy…The stars take over the sun's work, but with a dispassionate aloof coldness, like a frigid and beautiful stepmother taking over a nursery where once walked warm and true maternity. The earth itself stands like a child, awaiting the injustice and the blow."

As we listened to the radio that night, I knew the fruit was well developed, ready to be picked. In fact, as with the threat from Donna, there was an enormous investment in that crop. He listened to the report, analyzing what was being said. When they finished, he turned off the radio and said the now familiar, "Uh-huh."

Mama was astounded. She said, "Frank, what are you going to do?"

"I expect I'll go to bed."

"Aren't you worried, I mean, about the fruit freezing?"

"Well, I'll go to bed tonight like I always do. In the morning, I'll be richer or poorer. If the fruit freezes, we'll start over. If it doesn't, we'll sell it. Either way, I'll have something to do when I wake up."

As was his pattern, he slept like a baby that night, too.

I heard my mother say more than once that she would be happy with him if they lived in a tarpaper shack on a ditch bank and had to eat catfish and swamp cabbage. One time he told me, "Well, Buddy, it all belongs to the Lord, let him do as he pleases. Anyway, I figure we're just stewards of things he gives us. We don't really own anything." He never worried. He spent a lot of time figurin', but he didn't worry.

Clover Seed, Windows, Fists and Fencing

"I have never let my schooling interfere with my education."
-Mark Twain

I continued to work as usual while awaiting news from college admissions. It was the winter clover-planting time. There were vast pastures just east of the house that were ideal. Paw and Sonny had it all worked out to plant clover in with the established grasses. It would grow well, mix in with the grass and die out when it got hotter. During the time the clover was growing lush, the cows would have calved. They would need some supplementation to make extra milk for the babies. I didn't understand the big picture. The idea was to grow pounds of beef. Years later, I saw that what he said was true. Freshly calved cows didn't need clover or lush pasture during calving. They needed clover about four to six weeks afterwards, when the potential milk flow was greatest and the cows and babies would need extra nutrition. I remember seeing calves with the "clover scours". They would get a neonatal diarrhea from high volumes of rich milk and probably from nibbling on the clover as well. It was a temporary nutritional management disorder; we didn't do much about it. If the calf was healthy and vigorous, the policy was, "let him alone".

So one cool morning I went to the shop, finding that the old green Jeep had been rigged with a contraption called a seeder. The seeder was a five-gallon galvanized bucket affair held onto the front of the Jeep by braces and brackets. There was a paddle that spun on top of a motor under the seeder. This device worked well. You could set different flow rates for large seed or tiny clover seed, which was minuscule and black like poppy seed. So you had to lift the hood, attach the wires of the motor to the battery by clips and set the flow rate to approximate the amount of seed you wanted to apply to the pasture. We even made some "set runs" where we would put down newspaper or sheets, drive by at a constant speed and estimate the amount of seed that was scattered on the sheet. Once we worked out the flow rate and the speed, we could estimate how many pounds of seed per acre. It required a fast second gear, as I recall. The speed was critical. Too fast meant too little seed applied, while too slow meant over-application and wastage. There were a couple of 50-pound bags of clover seed and packets of inoculation media. The media was friendly bacteria that served as an activator of seed germination.

I put several pounds of clover seed into a five-gallon bucket and the prescribed amount of innoculum, stirred it thoroughly and poured it into the seeder. I attached the battery wires and took off. A quick jerk of a cord from the cab turned the seeder on, dropped the seed down onto the paddle and slapped it off in a twenty-five foot swathe. Paw made me some sticks to mark where I was aiming at each end of the pasture. I'd stay parallel with the fence to start, drive to the end of the pasture, get out and put a marker out for sighting the return trip. I'd put aluminum foil on squares of plywood and attached them to the sticks so I could see them. Some pastures were so big you barely could see a 12-inch square at the other end. The aluminum squares were a contrast to the green and visible. As I turned around, I could see the marker at other end. This way, I had a sight point to drive to. So I simply rode from marker to marker, moving them over so many paces at the end of each run. I could look and see my previous tire-tracks and judge my accuracy in driving parallel runs. This is the way we did it.

When you got through, you'd have driven in giant parallel zig-zags throughout the pasture. All this is to say that I didn't know what I was in for. I drove and drove and drove for what felt like months. The clover went a long ways. The green Jeep and I became well acquainted.

It took forever to seed a pasture. I remember singing to myself, talking (and answering myself), praying, whistling, and any other technique to keep from being bored. I got good at it. But, I guess the thing that got me was the constant jerking and jostling. The Jeep would hit the bumps, dipping and bouncing viciously from side to side. I hit my head on the cab several times, jarred my kidneys like a trucker and learned to drive hunkered over in the seat. Course, you can imagine what driving long days hunkered over does to your back and neck.

One day, several weeks later, as I was driving the iron maiden with the contraption on her nose, I realized I was reseeding a place. There in front of me were my tire-tracks and I was driving over them. I know how a pilot feels with moments of disorientation; however, I was on the ground. I made a quick swing to the right and got parallel to the tracks again, but that threw off the line of sight at the far end. This was the last straw; I had tried to do a good job but at last was defeated. I was furious at my incompetence. I was tired, butt-sore, lonely, cold and hungry. I just had to hit something. In a flash of anger I smashed the window of the Jeep with a balled up, gloved fist. The window looked like a shotgun had been fired into it. The safety glass held but it was smashed. I finished the day but was nonetheless chagrined.

The next morning, I was loading up what seemed like the thousandth bag of clover seed and the hundredth pound of inoculation media and up walked Paw. He rolled his cigar a little, inspecting the windshield.

Finally, he asked, "What happened to the window?"

"I hit it…"

(Pause)

"What did you hit it with?"

"My fist…"

(Another pause)

"Well, Boy, you'll have to pay for it."

"I expect to."

(Another longer pause while he rolled his cigar, thinking.)

"It's gonna cost 50 dollars and 50 cents." (I thought he surely was knowledgeable about windshield replacement prices.)

I gulped a little—that was a week's pay. "Okay."

He chuckled, "That'll be 50 cents for the windshield and 50 dollars for the hell of it."

I waited several months for the repair bill to arrive. It never came. I guess I still wait for that bill. The next day he put a block of wood with a crudely drawn bull's eye on it in the Jeep, between the seats. He said, "Boy, hit that when you just have to hit something." Unbeknownst to me, he had been the cause of the confusion and misjudgment. He was the one who drove through the pasture from corner to corner. His tire-tracks had thrown me off in my parallel driving. He went down to the seed store the next day and bought 4 more bags of clover and some Bahia grass seed. It took another month or two of shaking, rattling and rolling to put it out. I was sure glad to finish that job. It wasn't hard but it was tedious, requiring much self-discipline, which later served me well. And, I suppose that was the idea…

Fencing installation and repair went hand in glove with ranch and grove work. We had to dig holes for line-posts and gate-posts. Years ago during installation of telephone poles, men used long-handled posthole diggers, digging a deep hole, for the setting of a pole. The men who used these devices usually had strong chests and well developed shoulders and forearms. They'd lift the tool to the surface, bringing up a scoop of soil, and then would drive the blades back in with all the force they could muster. Little by little, the soil was removed and the hole dug to the appropriate depth. The pole or post was dropped in, followed by well tamped dirt or cement to secure it.

I never think of fence-building that I don't recall a funny episode: it brings back memories of pain, soreness and fatigue. Hubert and I installed a few gates and many fence posts. One particular time near the horse barn, we had two literd poles to set for the gateposts. They were 10 to 12 inches in diameter, twelve to fifteen feet long and must have weighed a ton. It generally took two men to set one this size in a hole. We'd have to stand it on end, then, if one man was rank enough, he would hug it like a Scottish pole tosser, lifting and walking straddle legged over the hole until centered, then drop it down, hoping that it was perfectly vertical so soil wouldn't fall in the hole and defeat the purpose of the deep seating of the post. The gateposts had to be big and heavy for the wire tension on them was tremendous. These heart of pine gateposts lasted for decades. The resinous sap was so concentrated and hard, almost petrified, that the staples would ricochet like bullets when you missed a hit with the hammer. You could lose an eye very quickly in that way. Also, we avoided "stack stapling". If the wire was under tension and you pounded a staple in on top of another, you could cut the wire, releasing it to take down a by-stander or two. We never worked with this wire without gloves; they were real skin savers.

So that particular day, Hubert and I were hanging tough with two heavy gateposts. He explained what we had to do. After the Camels got to him on the first hole, he turned the digging of the second one over to me. As I dug, he panted and chuckled, grumbling something like, "You long-winded son of a (*expletive deleted*)..." The holes had to be a few inches wider than the posts and about the depth of the handles of the diggers, which meant you'd end up digging the hole on your knees. Well I'd not gotten too far along when I tried a new technique—at least Hubert said it was new to him.

In an attempt to shove the digger deeply into the hole, I was really raring back and slamming it in as hard as I could. Only one problem: You must be careful <u>not</u> to let the scoops hit the edge of the hole with all your weight and momentum behind them. I was slamming down so hard, my body, and especially my head, was under tremendous momentum. The scoop portion of the diggers hit the side of the hole, stopping the diggers abruptly while my face kept its trajectory down and forward. As would be expected by the laws of physics that govern bodies in motion, I squarely centered an eye on each handle. The next day I looked like someone had gouged his thumbs in my eye sockets in a Zane Gray skull and knuckle fight. Hubert laughed so hard he had to sit down.

I was humbled that day...again. It only took this one time to teach me the finer points of post-hole digging.

Come On, Boy...I Need a Dozer Driver

"People who work sitting down get paid more than people who work standing up."
-Ogden Nash

DURING one of the early morning visits at the shop I heard the men talking about a new tractor. I had settled into the routine grove work by this time. Sure enough, one day a truck with a flatbed trailer pulled in with a brand new Caterpillar bulldozer on it. It was a small dozer, as dozers go, a "D-4". It was the most powerful thing I had inspected up close. They drove it over behind the cow pens and parked it. The next morning, Paw said, "Come on, Boy. I need a dozer driver." I swallowed hard. With me looking like a coon caught eating cat food, we went over to where the dozer was parked. He explained that I first had to lubricate all the fittings, then fire up the gasoline starting motor and pull a lever to engage the main diesel engine. I followed his instructions; it spit and coughed some but finally came to life. I disengaged the clutch and shut off the starter motor. Once the diesel was purring, I was ready for the warm up period. He showed me the hydraulics, the control levers, the blade control and several other things. I sat in the command seat of this marvelous monster as dark, sooty smoke bellowed from the stacks. I was in heaven. He got off the seat beside me and said, "Try it out. I want you to knock down all the trees in this pasture and the scrub bushes and pile them in big piles for burning. Leave those thick trees in the hammock and the brush for the birds and wildlife. Watch out for trees jumping over the blade and coming back at you. Drive in first or second gear." I tried it a little, started to push down small stuff and pile it up.

Deep in concentration I never noticed that he left me out there all alone. He didn't show up for a few hours. The old green Jeep came jostling back about quitting time. By then, I had knocked down and piled a small portion. I wasted motion some, but I was learning. He said, "How you doin', Buddy?" I said I was fine. We talked a little while about what the thing could do. I did the same thing the next day and many days thereafter. He moved me around some to various locations. I was getting better and better at it as the days went on.

Sonny would come by to check on me. He'd comment on the important things. Grease fittings were for daily lubrication of the key joints. He explained how to properly do this. He showed me other maintenance tips and how to avoid dangerous situations. He told me to listen to the machine – that it will talk to you if things aren't right. He warned me about a tree flipping over the blade and its whipping back on you in the cab. He said, "It will knock the taste out of your mouth." Hubert repeated many of these same things with me. He asked if my feet had gotten hot yet. I told him not yet. He said, "Well, a diesel works best when running a little hot. Don't let your rpm's drop. Keep it high and steady. The governor will cut in when you need extra power. Don't be worried about that, you'll know it when it happens. You'll know when it cuts in because it'll belch dark smoke and beller like a bull." He chuckled and said, "Boy, you ain't a dozer driver til you hav' to git your smoking boots off the floor of the cab. Put 'em on the dash and keep it moving, don't waste motion." This work went on for months. I'd get there early, grease 'er up while the engine warmed and pull out for trees and scrubs.

One late afternoon, Hubert came by on his way to the shop. He watched me a while, not saying a word. As it was about time to knock off work, I shut down and loaded my gear in the truck as Hubert went out to inspect the day's work. He wanted to talk and so did I. We leaned against his truck and talked idly while the day wound down. He recalled the times he drove a dozer for the county around Indiantown. He said he and his new bride, Vivian, moved to the woods, pulling a trailer behind a road grader. They unhitched and parked the trailer at a suitable spot and he went to grading road beds for the county. Later he was graduated to a D-8 dozer, a powerful eight-cylindered thing that moved lots of dirt in one swath. He laughed as he described the arrival of a new D-10. He related that there was a small crew of men working around a newly constructed bridge. Hubert was grading the road bed. Down the road a ways, the new pristine D-10 was unloaded off a flatbed trailer. The diesel smoke puffed as the driver wheeled it around to start the same work that Hubert was doing. Hubert said the man looked over at him and grinned.

The county's supervisor got in his truck and drove away down the finished portion of the road. As he cleared out of sight, Hubert and the D-10 driver had the same idea simultaneously: Would the two extra cylinders on the new dozer make any difference? Hubert snatched the steering lever, hit the brake to freeze the inside track for a short turn and pulled the throttle wide open. The other driver did much the same. They headed toward each other like two scrub bulls in a butting match. Out of each smoke stack, clouds of burnt diesel bellowed in dark acrid exhaust as the D-8 and the new D-10 monsters raced toward each other. They met in the middle of the sandy road in one loud clang of metal, coming to a dead stop. The tracks started digging into the soft sand and at first it was pure stalemate. The two bulls had locked horns and seemed equally matched. But Hubert said the D-10 began to bellow deep within its frame, sending vibrations through both machines. A billowing black cloud began to collect in the air over the D-10, moving only slightly in the soft breeze. The governors had cut in on the D-10. As Hubert explained, "governors" were the automatically activated throttles that increased power when the machine hits a heavy load or burden. "Once the governor cut in, I couldn't do a thing with him. My tracks just dug in the sand as he began to slowly push me backwards. We wallered out a hole big enough to park a truck in…The fella just laughed at me…I wadn't gonna let that son of a (*expletive deleted*) git away without knowin' what that D-10 could do…Boy, he jus' took it away from me…" They backed out of their manmade bull holes, covered up the evidence and went back to work.

About the time I got comfortable with clearing pasture, I was told to take the dozer to a different location where it seemed I was to have a new job chopping the old pastures. What in the world was "chopping"? It was rather simple, however. The chopper is best described as a water tank turned on its side with thick, sharp metal cleats welded to it, radiating out like a giant rolling pin with cutter blades on it, held by a big frame that attaches to the hitch of the tractor. When weighted with water, the chopper was an awesome device. So you pulled this rolling cutter behind the tractor at a fairly good pace and the pasture sod is cut and aerated. You just rolled over small scrub trees, rank palmettos and small brush. It whacked them into 12-inch pieces. It felt like you were on board ship with the soft rolling motion of the dozer. I used a much higher gear in this activity. It was action-packed and rewarding. You could look behind you and see where you'd been. My feet got hot.

I asked Mama to fix me iced tea and sandwiches for dinner. Hubert said that the best thing to do was keep moving. He said, "A dozer makes money moving, not idling or shut off." I didn't know any better and took him at his word. Driving through the dinner break, I tried eating while I drove, with the constant sound of the diesel vibrating the metal cage, the smell of hot fumes and the blistering floor. I never managed to master drinking ice tea from a thermos jug while running wide open in third gear. It kept sloshing out on my shirt. That was not all bad; however, since a wet shirt gave me some relief from the heat. This trick of evaporative cooling was common before ice became available. You would see wooden water jugs with a thick layer of hemp sacks tied over them. When you got a drink, you'd splash a little water on the top of the sacks. The evaporation kept the water cool and pleasant.

There is something very satisfying about knowing that you are doing good work. All young men should experience this success. During these days and weeks, Paw said nothing. Then one night at supper, he idly commented to Reeda, "Mama, I think the ol' boy is making a dozer driver." That was all – but I never had such an encouragement. I realized that he was not one to give unwarranted praise and that a few words well placed were worth many poorly chosen.

Another rung in my ladder of self esteem had been mounted.

Dogs Seemed to be Part of the Family

"When I carefully consider the curious habits of dogs, I am compelled to conclude that man is the superior animal. When I consider the curious habits of man, I confess, my friend, I am puzzled."
-Ezra Pound

ALONG about the time I was well settled into the routines of ranch work, we added a Weimaraner, named Hans, to the ranch's "canine crew." Smokey had died of kidney disease and Dot of old age. Hans had taken up with Dot's puppy, Billy Sol Estes and Shorty, who was senile by this time. Billie Sol's back legs were slightly crooked, thus his name. You might remember a scandal about that time surrounding President Johnson and a Texas scoundrel in some shady dealings.

The dogs had worked out their pecking order. Hans was younger and the leader. He was special because he could come into the house evenings. He owned a folded blanket on the hearth, just next to Paw's green recliner.

One evening the preacher of a local church came out to the ranch, accompanied by a deacon. He mentioned that they were planning a new church building and they would appreciate any financial help that my parents could offer. Mother had served her famous pecan pie. The preacher happened to be sitting in the recliner and had just made his appeal. Now, it was deer hunting season and we had just processed a deer at the shop that morning. Hans had been there, eating the tidbits of fresh venison. We'd toss some to all the dogs as we skinned the deer. He'd had his share and more besides.

I don't know if you know about dogs eating a full load of fresh deer meat, but it causes a terrible gas problem. Apparently the bacteria in the lower colon set about final biochemical fermentation on the residues that survive the gastric and enzymatic hydrolysis. The result is a colon filled with a rank and odiferous, methanogenic mass. That's probably more than you wanted to know, but at that critical moment when the preacher began his final appeal, Hans began to expel the eye-watering fumes close beside him. It was all very subtle and quiet, but deadly. If you watched real closely, you could see his tail lift just slightly every now and then. When Mama detected the phenomenon she said, "Frank, put Hans outside."

He growled from the other side of the room, "Aw, leave him alone." This same exchange was repeated a couple more times. The preacher sat forward an inch at a time until he was perched on the front edge of the chair, elbows on knees, I suppose trying to distance himself from the ever expanding gas pocket. The discussion continued in greatly abbreviated form with Hans making an occasional contribution. Finally, he could take it no longer and, with a gratifying and generous commitment of support from Mama and Paw, stood up to leave. We all shook hands.

When they were gone, Mama scolded Paw for leaving Hans in the house with the gas problem. He belatedly got up and clicked to Hans who eagerly followed him. As Hans started out the door, Paw looked down and softly said, "Hans, you're a good dog." Hans paused, gazed up at him with what I swear was a grin, sneezed, wagged his stubby tail and walked into the night. I'll never forget that sight. Paw had that twinkle in his eye, one that I grew to relish. You see he just had a knack for handling people, preachers, dogs and wealth.

Hans

HANS was truly a remarkable dog. He was all velvet gray, had gray-yellow eyes and about a 5″ long tail. He was my introduction to a multi-use working dog. He hunted birds, ran deer, foxes, raccoons, otters and anything else with fur or feather. He would hunt feral hogs. (He was like me in that endeavor, he'd do it but he wasn't really very good at it.) We saw him run down a turkey one day. As the bird lifted off the ground in flight, Hans leapt up and grabbed him by the tail. He and the turkey tumbled butt over teakettle. The turkey got away. Hans returned spitting out a mouthful of sticky feathers, but pleased with himself.

When he was jogging beside the green Jeep, sort of in a trance, you'd think he wasn't paying attention, but if something stirred up ahead or to the side, he'd shift into a powerful gallop that sounded like a small horse. He'd come by you wide open like a greyhound. He was a marvel to watch. He ran 15 to 25 miles almost every day and was as tough as nails. He'd plunge into the cool water of ponds or canals as we drove by them, submerge his body and drink great gulps for a few intense seconds. Then off he'd go to catch up to or pass the Jeep. Sundays irritated him if we didn't take a ride. I understand that thoroughbreds in an excellent state of physical condition get "antsy" when they don't go for a daily run. Apparently, when muscles are toned to perfection, there is a need for continued exercise. I think Hans was that way. He'd bounce all over the yard when we would come out to the Jeep, bark his delight and impatience, jog off a little ways, turn and look at us as if to say, "What's the problem? Let's go!"

One morning Paw came out as usual; Hans was all excited and did his routine dance at seeing his master. Paw liked to pause and smell the air some. He'd stand and roll his cigar, look at the sky and clouds, gazing off into the distance as if he was analyzing something, getting the feel of the day. Some of his best problem solving was done at 10 mph in that old green Jeep with the dogs or grandkids riding or jogging alongside him.

Well, this particular morning it was colder than kraut and Hans was more than raring to go. Paw was little slower than usual, perhaps teasing the eager dog a bit. When Hans had had enough, he reached up and nipped him in the butt. Paw whirled around and kicked at him. He missed and, slipping on loose pebbles, fell down on the offended rear end, right there just outside the garage.

Mama heard the grumbling and cursing. She came out just in time to see him get up, straighten his sunglasses, adjust his hat, and look for his cigar.

"Frank, what are you doing?" she asked.

"I'm trying to kick the (*expletive deleted*) out of this dog. He bit me in the butt."

She went back in the house smiling. It was just another day in paradise.

There are a few more dogs that come to mind. There was Cookie and Belle, Sonny and Betty's kids' dogs. The reason I remember Cookie so well was because Sonny and I tried to get the ticks off her with gasoline. We were cleaning a tractor part with a pan of gas and an old rag. I happened to see Cookie standing nearby. She had a tremendous tick on the back of her neck. Sonny idly daubed a spot of gasoline on it and the tick soon fell off. I am sure that this method of tick removal is not an acceptable one, but at the time we didn't think of that.

On closer inspection we saw a few more ticks on her neck and daubed a little gas on them, too. Well sir, we found a few more and daubed. We looked her over close and found that she was absolutely covered in small ticks. Bending over her, we proceeded to daub them all, a few here, a few, there, until we had pretty much covered her all over. We noticed that she began to squirm a little. Being a cur dog, we figured she could just tough it out. What finally occurred to us was that she was miserable; her skin was on fire from the gas. We finally let her go. She bee-lined it to a pond and dove in. She wallowed in the mud and water and finally came out, much relieved. We allowed that we wouldn't do that again; it was a little harsh. From then on, if she so much as smelled gas she would pull out for the nearest pond.

Belle was a little different, more like a boxer than a cur dog. She had a "burnt face", as we called it, as if she had stuck her muzzle in soot. It is possible they were half-sisters, since you would not have believed they were sisters at first glance. She lived longer than Cookie and I think she got a little meaner in old age. The kids loved them. As I recall, neither was much of a cow dog.

Sonny got a Rhodesian Ridge-back, though I forget his name. He was proud of this dog; it was an African dog used to run lions. Partner commented, "Y'all 'spect we need to start watchin' for lions 'round here?" This beast didn't tolerate other dogs well. There would be a dogfight every morning as they set about to re-establish the pecking order—as dogs will do. For some reason, the Rhodesian renegade never accepted the truce that had been made the previous morning. Every new dog, male or female, was fair game for a challenge. He would be top dog, or else. One day, Hubert drove up to the shop with a long-nosed English bulldog riding in the truck. He got out and the dog jumped out, too. The Ridgeback couldn't stand that so he attacked. Well, the bulldog was not too impressed about being accosted by this beautiful red beast. There was a heated exchange and the Ambassador from Rhodesia suddenly realized he'd made a serious blunder with the Prime Minister of England. They settled the issue with the bulldog getting high honors in the debate. Hubert called the bulldog, loaded him back in the truck and took him back to the place he borrowed him from. As I recall, that ended the daily fighting for a while. Hubert said, "I was afraid the bulldog would kill him, but I took a chance. I don't think Sonny would appreciate his dog gettin' killed, but I was tired of that son of a (*expletive deleted*) jumping on everything every morning."

Hubert had a dog named Jake. He was solid and mostly brindle with some white and black spots. He was obviously a mixed bulldog and cow dog cross. He had a blocky head and big chest; I expect he weighed about 70 pounds. He was well conditioned and a bit mean. Like most cow dogs, you didn't mess with them. They were working dogs and didn't take to cuddling. I liked to work with them since they were tough and pain tolerant. Jake was a marvel to watch when he was tuned-in on working cattle. He'd head them off, turn them, bring back escapees from the herd, and grab the nose of aggressive ones. As the cowboys would have said it, "A bull would sure pay the price if he showed his country behind in front of Jake."

One day, a calf escaped the herd, pulling out for parts unknown. Jake saw him and quickly turned away to intercept. He caught the calf and began a systematic biting of ears and nose. He circled him like a wolf on a downed elk. I couldn't break it up. He had reverted to absolute meanness at that point. As I was hazing him, trying to get between him and the target of his aggression, Hubert rode in at full gallop uncoiling his rope, cut the dog away, and, riding hard on his tail, roped him. He got off his horse and proceeded to stomp the stuffings out of Jake's head, holding a back leg. I thought he would kill him. Jake tried to bite Hubert several times and this only brought down more wrath. When Hubert finished the lesson for the day, he took off the rope, careful to watch his hand, turned the dog loose and ordered, "Now get behind me!" Jake just shook it off as if it was the cost of doing business and fell in behind his master. He worked perfectly from that time to the end of the long day. Hubert explained, "He jus' needs his ears cleaned out every now and then. If I don't do that, he'll kill something. He's got a mean streak that needs adjusting sometimes." I now recognize that dogs only appreciate a dominant pack leader. Hubert and Jake had an understanding; Hubert was the lead dog! (My observation: A happy dog is not a fat dog; it is one who has work to do, is tired from it, and has a leader to follow.)

The last time I saw Jake, he was sitting in the front seat of Hubert's car with all the air conditioning ducts turned toward him. He was a little gray around the muzzle; so was Hubert. "That ol' dog worked hard his whole life. He can sit in the front seat with me from now on." That was high praise from Hubert. He appreciated one who took care of business; he didn't appreciate stupidity or laziness. There was a line you didn't cross. When he sensed the crossover, he'd call you on it. He was a tough man, owning tough dogs, coming from tough times, but a man of simple honor and loyalty, nonetheless, able to stomp man or beast into submission if the need arose.

Our dogs frequently jumped in the back of the Jeep for a rest on the long rides. Hans had a bad habit of cold-nosing you behind the ear and knocking your hat askew. Paw would grumble, cutting his eyes at Hans. Hans would give him a silly grin; they understood each other without words being exchanged. If Hans and Billie got in a heated discussion about who was to sit closest to Paw, he would take off his hat, flap at both of them in the middle of their argument and grumble something like, "Git the (*expletive deleted; place of doomed departed)* outta here!" They'd both clear out and, while running alongside the Jeep, continue their squabbling rivalry. This hat beating would also occur when the dogs jumped back into the Jeep and a blast of skunk or dead carcass odor accompanied them or they had severe gas problems. Paw couldn't take that either. He'd swat indiscriminately around in the back. Billie would sometimes suck back in a corner, rolling his eyes. Hans would leave. This hat method worked well for thick mosquitoes, wasps, bees, squabbling dogs and squabbling kids, too.

That old Stetson hat was not exactly the latest style but it was a good hat. He wore it until it was grubby and sweat-stained. Nobody knew how long. It really looked bad. Mama decided, after suggesting several times that he buy a new one, to do it herself, which she did. She hung the new hat on the hat rack in the garage and took the old one out to the garbage dump with the trash. She set fire to the pile, and came home thinking that-was-that. Paw came in later and asked where his hat was. She explained what she had done. He graciously resigned himself to the breaking in of a new hat. The next day, to her surprise and dismay, he came in wearing the old hat and chuckling. Hans had retrieved it, laying it in the driver's seat of the Jeep where he figured it belonged. It had been burned on one side of the brim. I didn't know if Hans pulled it out of the fire or if it fell off the pile before it burned up. I never thought about catching him to look close to see if his muzzle hairs were singed.

Paw wore it until Mama took it off somewhere and disposed of it. She would not tell us where she took it. I think she buried it. Knowing her, I expect she had a few words to say over it. Years later, after he had passed away, she cried and laughed over the memory of that hat. She carried the new Stetson hat in the rear window of the Cadillac for years. She said it sent a message that she wasn't traveling alone. In a way, she wasn't.

Shug

"The business dog has his own ear marks. He is self-contained. He expects no luxuries of life, no graciousness. He possesses usually a simple integrity. He does his work faithfully and well and takes his pan of cornbread and an occasional bone, not with gratitude, but with the dignity of one who knows he has earned, that day, his keep. His gratitude is reserved for the rare expression of friendliness.
-Marjorie Kinnan Rawlings

OF all the dogs I've known there was one who made such an impact on my younger life that she deserves her own chapter. Actually, she was the daughter of a bloodhound given to me by Hubert, Old Beulah. She was toothless, had sagging udders from multiple litters and was as sweet as the day is long. She had been a tracking dog for the Clewiston Chain Gang in her younger days. She ended up as a brood bitch for more bloodhound puppies to train. You could not take her on an overnight camping trip and she would walk the palmettos all night looking for something to trail. Paw said she could blow the cobwebs out of a deer track and tell how many weeks ago he went by. It would drive me nuts listening to her rustle around in the night, smelling with that vacuum cleaner nose of hers.

By the time I got her, she was a little worn out and old. I liked her just fine. I was working for a veterinarian in Gainesville, Florida, at the time. He had an English bulldog named Butch. Well, old Butch and Beulah hit it off. Someone said he must have used a Miami phone directory to stand on when he bred her. Anyway, Beulah had six fine crossbred puppies. I kept one; called her Shug. She was a light red with a broad head and thick chest. Her south end had a little to be desired in bulk, but from the lumbar region forward, she was heavy and well-muscled. I trained her to follow hand commands. She wanted to catch things on command but didn't ever know what to do with them once she had them. She learned that "Yip....Catch'im" meant take him down by the nose. I suspect that this was instinctual from the bulldog bloodlines. At first she really got in the way while working cattle.

She just couldn't figure it out. She had been reared away from other cattle dogs and had no models for technique, until one day when it all came together. I'll never know if it was the threat she felt for me or sheer instinct that took control. In either case, I owe a lot to that old dog. Don't misunderstand, she never was a world-class cow dog, but that day she became the closest thing to a real catch dog that I'll ever own.

We had a problem with grove cows. These cattle slipped the fence or found a place to enter a grove and would get as fat as town dogs on the fertilized grasses. They got smart, too, and could avoid attempts to get them out of their havens. They'd dart under trees, making it impossible to rope them even if you were good at it. It was no mean feat to get them out, especially the experienced ones. Well, we divided up into searchers in the grove we called "The Four Hundred" where a smart cow lived. Hubert went one way, someone else went another direction. I was alone in the southwest section. Easing down the rows looking, approaching the back fence where a big oak shaded part of the grove, I rode right up on her. Shug was trotting along behind me. The cow snorted a little and ran under some trees for cover. Shug stood there as if deciding what to do next. I rode the renegade cow out into the middle between two rows of trees, and was nearly knocked off the horse by the tree limbs. I could get her out but it was like trying to pile ants to keep her out from under the trees. She was a skilled escape artist, having practiced a good bit on failed attempts to move her out to the pasture.

After several tries she'd had enough and came after me, determined to rid herself of this annoyance. She had handlebar horns, you know, like the handlebars of a customized Harley motorcycle. She nearly got me and my horse a couple of times. I guess I looked like a mounted picador at the bullfights. I needed help and I needed it fast. I yelled for Hubert and "yipped" and "yipped". Finally, in some desperation, I called to Shug, "Catch'im!" Apparently at that point she got the message. Her instincts kicked in and she went at that cow, first trying to bite her horns, which didn't work, but finally catching her by the nose. The cow would have none of it. She slung her tormentor from side to side, bouncing her body off horns and trees. The weight difference had to be 1300 to 80. Shug lost her grip once and went back "to git anuther holt", as the Crackers called it. The cow tossed her off a time or two, but Shug wouldn't quit. She repeatedly went into the jaws of hell and caught her target again and again. This last time, when the cow just barely missed goring her, Shug clamped on the nose, holding her tight. I found out what the heavy chest was for. It was for lateral movement. She latched onto the cow and held her until the cow gave up. It couldn't have been more than a few minutes but felt like an eternity. My horse was bouncing around wanting to bolt out from the tight quarters. The cow came out from under the orange trees bellowing and dragging that dog between her front legs. Shug was balled up with legs drawn in tight.

I watched in horror as the cow stepped right on Shug's abdomen. She whimpered some but held on. I knew she was badly injured and tried to call her off. I was sure her intestines had been mashed or her spleen ruptured. But she would not quit. The cow was exhausted, gasping for breath, "Get this thing off my nose." I rode up beside the cow and put a rope on her horns. Shug and I drug her out of the grove to the main road way as Hubert arrived. We then had double ropes on her.

I had to get off my horse to convince Shug that it was all over. As I approached, I saw the muscles ripple in the top of her head. Her eyes were half closed. She was re-setting her grip. After a little encouragement, she rolled her eyes at me as if to say, "After all the trouble I went to to catch this beast, are you sure you want me turn her loose?" But she dropped off and went behind me.

The cow charged me again and that dog went back to work, using the skill she had just perfected.

I finally got Shug off and away. She was exhausted. I had to cool her off in a nearby pond. "She mite near had the thumps" (the Cracker expression for the extremely fast breathing indicating imminent heat stroke). I didn't have any way to carry her to Doc Platt, so we headed back with Shug beside my horse. Outside the grove gates, Hubert whipped his stiff lariat off the cow's horns and she trotted off into the woods outside the grove. She'd had enough.

It was a long ride back that afternoon, knowing my dog was probably dying. I expected her to give up on the way, but as we drew closer to the barn, she wasn't showing any signs of distress. I'd wait on her at every pond or water hole. She'd walk in, sink down into the cool water up to her back, and lap great quantities of water. She was sore the next day but never complained nor showed any sign of serious damage. I never figured how we got out of that train wreck without one of us being badly hurt or killed.

Hubert came to me one day, not long after that and asked if he could borrow Shug. I asked why. He said he had a tight-jawed bull that needed an education and Shug was just the one who could educate him. In a little while they came back. Shug was hot but unhurt. I swear she looked proud of herself.

In 1968, Paw said Shug just didn't come home one day after a round of Jeep riding. We never knew exactly what happened to her. The ranch was a big place. We think she was killed by a rattler, got too hot, or run over by a piece of heavy grove equipment at a Ft. Drum grove. She was friendly to people, so she could have gotten lost, found and moved in her suitcase with another family. I hope that is what happened. She was a good dog. I still miss her. Not the smartest I've seen, nor the strongest, nor was she the most gifted, she was, however, the best friend a boy could have. She did the very best she could with her gifts and ability. Enthusiastically loyal, she treated me like she'd not seen me for years every time I came home, even if it had only been 30 minutes or even when I was ill tempered for some reason that day. She was truly an example of unconditional love, salve for a healing heart.

Florida Cur Dogs

"Dogs display reluctance and wrath
if you try to give them a bath.
They bury bones in hideaways
and half the time they trot sideways."
-Ogden Nash, *"An Introduction to Dogs"*, in *I'm a Stranger (1938)*

IT is a vast understatement to say the life of cow dogs and catch dogs is hard. They remind me of the Alaskan sled dogs. People think they are mistreated by their harsh life style. The truth is they have no greater joy than to do what is their calling. To them, a trip running twenty to thirty miles in front of a snow-covered sled in 20 degree below-zero blizzards is worth begging for.

A cow dog can be a threat to strangers; these dogs don't take kindly to them. I've gotten bayed-up more than once by a pack of yard dogs when I approached a house or cow pens. Wayne Collier's dogs would lie in wait under the house. You had to toot the horn and call before you got out. Mrs. Collier, his mother, would come to the door and say, "It's okay. Let him alone." They'd go back to sleep. Fred Hartt's cur dog, for example, would lie in wait, softly move in behind you, then suddenly bite you in the butt or legs. Suzie's bite left a Technicolor bruise that would remain for days. I carried red-pepper spray for her. But in their element, doing what they were bred to do, they were truly marvelous to watch.

Florida cur dogs are working dogs. They weren't generally friendly or used to petting. You know the old dog-training rule: Exercise first, discipline next, then affection. Pervert that sequence and you'll have some problems. Well, active cur dogs didn't have to have exercise; they worked all day along beside the horses. Discipline was needed sometimes because they could get a little rough. Sometimes it was a fine line between being a killer and being rough. After all, going up against a 1300-pound mean bull, weighing only 70 pounds is considered by some to be a suicide mission. They'd try it though. Convincing determined cattle to return to the herd took skill and courage. They worked better in a group. There was at times a young dog in the bunch for on-the-job training. Some of them got killed or suffered broken bones, but most picked up their skill by watching the experienced dogs. Just like the wolf pack, they worked with instinctual understanding, but the wolf instinct was tamed down a bit to herd cattle and not kill them. A few would revert to pure meanness but most of these dogs were strictly business types. I am surprised that only a few went too far.

Some Florida cow dogs not only worked cattle but were accomplished at catching feral hogs. Many were cut by boar's tusks, some killed by them. It was not unusual for a man to suture up his dog with fishing line, cotton thread, or some other fine material on the tailgate of his truck, without any anesthetic. Though more than one hog hunter has had a tooth hung in his forearm, hand or elbow when the needle hit a tender place. Tough, ah thank…. One of them said, "When you tie the knots on fishing line, tie a knot for ever' day you want 'im to stay stitched up…" The dogs thought it was just the price of admission to a hog hunting trip, I guess.

They were heavy-chested, usually dark red or brindle but some were speckled or even all white. Marvelously conditioned and thickly muscled, they were not as big as you'd think. Some weighed upwards toward 60-70 pounds but the extremely muscled ones were subject to heat stroke. Many were in the 50-60 pound range, lean, tough and mean. Not many were fat, at least for very long anyway. Some had white areas or spots on them or the neck was encircled with white, thus the name, "ring-necked cur". Occasionally, there were those who had "burnt" faces, like a Boxer's face. Some looked like they had bulldog in their bloodlines. Many were line bred, meaning that close relatives were in their bloodlines. Some were frankly inbred, being from father-to-daughter type breeding or some such arrangement. I recall one such inbred dog brought into the clinic one time. He was a little pig-eyed, having eyes of different colors and no pigment around the lid of one of them. This dog was jumpy, nervous, hyper-sensitive and more than a little erratic. He would snap at imaginary bugs. I mentioned to his owner, "This dog acts a little inbred, don't he?"

"Yeah Doc, he is. He's so danged inbred, he's his own uncle!"

Well-trained or especially gifted cur dogs were very desirable for the work they did and the time they saved. I heard of a Seminole who by himself took herds of woods cattle to the sale in Ft Pierce, some 30-40 miles away, just him and two dogs. These were not your tame Herefords or Angus, they were wild woods cattle. It is said that the dogs could read his mind. He'd approach a gate in a pasture fence, the dogs would keep the cattle bunched next to the fence while the man rode in, opened the gate and went on through. The dogs not only brought them through the gate but would go ahead and slow the stampede to a walking bunch again.

In later years I patched up many cow dogs. The cowboys would invariably ask me, "When kin we use 'im agin?" I'd say something funny, like, "Well, pretend like your guts have been stomped out for half a day and you just had them washed and replaced. How long would you need to rest?" They got the message. The ranch wives usually took care of them. I kept some dogs at the clinic for several extra days, "forgetting" to call for pick up because I knew the son of a gun would not stay home if a horse left the barn. I guess there's a lesson in these cow dogs for all of us: when you find out what you're good at, stay with it.

As a friend once told me, "Half of success is showing up—the remaining 80% is working at it."

The Author at 18

Learning to Love the Woods

"Life went through the moss-hung forest, the swamp, the cypresses, through the wild sow and her young, through me, in its continuous chain. We were all one with the silent pulsing. This was the thing that was important, the cycle of life, with birth and death merging, one into another in an imperceptible twilight and an insubstantial dawn. The universe breathed, and the world inside it breathed the same breath."
-Marjorie Kinnan Rawlings, in *Cross Creek*

MY limited experience as a Florida woodsman made me at first a little self-conscious. Because of that I slipped off by myself after work, on the week-ends or later during breaks from college. These walk-abouts were usually with a dog or two. Many times I took the green Jeep or any available vehicle to a remote place, as far as I could take it on an old trail. I'd park, get out and wander the woods to see what I could see. Sometimes the underbrush acted as a barrier; it also was a lot of work to get through these tangles.

I camped at various spots. The best time was winter; it was cold, but the mosquito population was low. In the summers they swarmed in tremendous numbers. Sleeping in the woods, especially in the wet season, could be a touch of hell on earth. But I had not discovered anything new. What sparked my need to be alone in my discoveries were twofold: firstly, this was marvelous country that just needed to be explored; and, secondly, the stories Paw told about pioneer Florida. His vivid memories created a longing in my soul…His reminiscences in the Jeep, on a boat or at a campfire, ignited a need in me to feel, see and taste the woods. Alone in the deep woods at night, I went over and over these stories. Unconsciously, I might have known that my world would ultimately expand beyond this life. I guess I wanted to breathe in as much of it as I could.

Having been raised in the woods, Paw had exceptional woodsman skills. On our last bird-hunting trip together, he shot a big rattlesnake on the cow trail. I don't know how many had walked by it, not even seeing it. He told me to know where I was walking, to step a few steps and look down to see if the way is clear. I do this today, thinking unconsciously about it. It's funny how you develop certain habits in the woods.

I'd hunt for a campfire spot in the late afternoon, letting the dogs run free. Oak hammocks, cabbage palm islands, sandbars on creeks or pine thickets near ponds were good sites for a camp. There was usually firewood scattered nearby. Dead oak wood made a good fire. Literd pine knots would burn even when wet if you could get them hot enough. I made the coffee by pouring grounds into boiling creek- or pond-water. You'd have to let it set a few minutes and then add some cool water to settle the grounds out. If you were careful, you could pour a cup with only a few grains in it. When you got near the bottom of the pot, though, you'd be drinking more grounds than coffee. That's why you never drank camp coffee in a hurry. You waited until it had a chance to settle. Somehow it was delicious, even if you had to pick grounds out of your teeth. There was something comforting about just sitting there in the dark, smelling the smoke and watching the fire, listening to the night sounds and boiling coffee water. In the dark, noise carries a long way, especially in cold weather, especially over bodies of water. You could hear a turkey call at twilight, a buck snorting alarm, an armadillo rustling up a meal, a Bobcat's squawl or the cry of some poor victim in something's teeth.

The dogs would pull out for parts unknown, hunting and sniffing the wonderful smells that only dogs appreciate. They'd return to camp sporadically to see if I had moved. I'd hear one taking up a chase of some unlucky creature. Then all the dogs would join in as soon as they could locate the activity. I could identify them by their voices. They gave up when whatever it was they chased escaped. The dogs were pretty tired when they came in to lie by the fire; however, they never fully relaxed. They would listen to the night sounds, eyes closed, ears back. Then one, followed by all, would perk up, listening intently, sometimes followed by a low deep rumbling growl. Was it danger? A threat? Then, as if on some signal, they would relax back into their snoozing vigil. They slipped out like Army Rangers, there one moment, evaporated the next. It was marvelous to watch their natural behavior. I grew to appreciate their abilities and learned woods-sense from them. Dogs sometimes got lost or separated. Hunters would build a big fire, laying their hunting jacket nearby on the ground. When they returned the next day, the lost dogs would be waiting near that jacket.

Cows and calves walked right up to camp, particularly if I was located near a trail. They'd stop, perk up their heads, flare their nostrils and sniff the air. If I didn't move, they'd work their ears back and forth trying to pick up identifying signs. The whole line would stop and stare like cars passing a wreck. This quiet appraisal lasted for several minutes. The calves would keep moving up the line to view the reason for the sudden standstill. It took time for them to learn the tricks of the trade. If I moved or spoke, they'd snort-blow an alarm, startled into running off a short distance, stop and whirl around to take another look. But if unalarmed, they'd just amble off. It was rare for one of them to get aggressive. Maybe a bull would approach for a closer look. These weren't the aggressive outlaw cattle that are described in Western pioneer history. They didn't hunt you up like some wild cattle will. It was a game of sorts for me to see if I could remain undetected.

Wildlife

FEW people know about or have experienced the woods world of
Florida up close. This is more than ever a gold mine of memories for me. It
was apparent, even this early in life, that I was living in a wildlife paradise. On
these camping trips and walkabouts, I surprised many a creature and have
been most thoroughly cursed by startled squirrels and whooping cranes.
And I have been startled in turn. A Sand Hill Crane can fly fairly quietly. And if
you happen to be near a clump of trees or brush, and they fly right over your
head, their sudden distinctive alarm calls will scare the living daylights out
of you. I've heard that an owl can fly undetectably. It has to do with the wing
feather design. One fella told me once that an owl swooped in on his hat in
the dark. It was a light colored Stetson. Mr. Owl mistook it for something to
eat, I guess.

I remember seeing turkey, owls, blue herons, egrets (cow herons),
snipe, eagles, red-tailed hawks, bobwhite quail, doves and all kinds of water-
fowl. Cormorants or "water turkeys" were long-necked diving birds whose
feathers easily became waterlogged. You'd see them on the banks or on
limbs near water with their wings spread out to sun-dry. They were excellent fishers.

Occasionally you'd see pond skimmers, streaking across the water with
the lower bills set just at the surface. But they were more common nearer
the coast. There is a particular call of a pond bird I can remember today. It
is probably a member of the piper family. It was heard mostly at dusk when
they were startled into flight. You could hear the quail calls in the afternoons
and at dusk, and at daylight, ducks whistling by overhead in the cool air.
They made a whooshing sound as they set their wings for landing. Many
water fowl made noises as they flew.

Robert Butler's painting of "The Oak of Compassion"

At dusk most birds roosted. They would fly in loose formations to their perches for the night. Turkey would flap their wings vigorously to get their heavy bodies off the ground, going nearly straight up into the tallest pines they could find. If you returned before daylight, you could attend their rising. They'd pull their heads out from under their wings, look all around, ruffle their feathers and follow by a squirt of turkey manure that splat-hit a cabbage palm fan or the ground. They'd look around for a suitable period of time and, as if on cue, fly down and collect into a loose group. Then, off they'd go, serenely looking for breakfast.

When I drove out at night, I'd see night hawks, or what was called "bull bats" because of the peculiar low humming call they gave as they darted through the air, catching insects. As the lights of the Jeep hit them in the road or trails, their eyes shone like Christmas tree lights. They'd dart off on long graceful pointed wings as you approached them.

Florida was heaven for carrion eaters. Buzzards patrolled most of the ranch. They had favorite roosts and the stench underneath was awful. Wildlife specialists say they are really a clean bird. I don't know where they got this. One Cracker told me of the time a buzzard flew into the windshield of his truck. It stuck there, entangled in the wiper blades. He got out to remove the danged thing and it suddenly vomited on him and the hood of his truck. Whatever dead thing this buzzard had just eaten was ripe. "Son," he exclaimed, "use a stick or something when you move one of them things; that stuff is rank. Ya' better wash off yer truck too or the paint will peel off wher' it throwed up..." Most Cracker boys soon learn that you don't want buzzard vomit on your clothes.

Otters were a joy to watch. They'd play while they hunted, tumbling in mock fights, cackling to each other in otter-speak. They'd try this pond or that canal, cross over to another waterway. They made little mudslides on the canal banks where they would over and over again slide down and then skitter back up for another pass. The dogs would try to catch them but found that an otter is a terrible thing to grab. They roll around in their skins and bite a dog a half-dozen times before he can let go. Hans learned this valuable life lesson. His head abscessed and his wounds drained for two weeks.

I was lying on a tarp one morning beside a canal, watching a deer herd at daylight. It was deathly quiet when I heard all this chattering/laughing behind me. There was splashing, squabbling, and "pluke-noises" as two otters made their way down the waterway to their favorite crossing, which happened to be about fifteen feet from me. Well, here they came, up the bank and over the dike, piling nose-to-tail, right up beside me. They suddenly spotted me and stopped abruptly, stone still. We looked at each other for a couple of split seconds. They were the first to blink. They tossed mud, dirt, and grass three feet high as they scrambled to make their escape. Halting about fifteen yards away, they turned, curious to look me over at a circumspect distance. One eyed the other, as if to say, "Son! Whatever that is sure is ugly...Let's get out of here!" And on synchronized gesture, they were on their way down the dike like giant gray caterpillars, otter-talking away in the early dawn.

Raccoons, 'possums, gray and fox squirrels, field rats and mice shuffled around at various times of the day or night. There were gopher tortoises, land terrapins and snapping turtles around. The Crackers called the tortoises "gopher turtles" or "scrub chicken" when they were fried for dinner. These gentle creatures, now protected, didn't bother anyone much but they did make burrows in the ground up to thirty-feet long. Armadillos and rattlers used these holes, too. It wasn't unusual to find a rattler and gopher in the same hole. They tolerated each other. The gopher holes were great for little creatures hiding from woods or prairie fires, but hell on the legs of running horses. The old gophers were miniature versions of the Galapagos Island tortoises. They meandered around ponderously, eating grass and undergrowth, mostly minding their own business.

Snapping turtles were a different thing altogether. They usually stayed in the water, but, on occasion, would pull out for new pools and waters, driven for food or sex, much like alligators, I expect. You'd see them out in the middle of a pasture, waddling along on some errand. They could take off a finger with their sharp beaks. Some grew to be huge and were a rod-breaking experience for the unlucky fisherman that hooked one.

There were all varieties and sizes of snakes. I saw eastern diamondback rattlesnakes, coral snakes and non-poisonous imitators, water moccasins, copperheads, and water snakes of various species. You had to watch your step in some wet places. Water snakes were bad to lie in ambush on overhanging limbs in the creeks. Black snakes, king snakes, rat snakes, green snakes and yellow snakes inhabited most of the haunts of vermin. Many amphibians were native. All kinds of frogs populated the waters. Little green tree frogs were everywhere in cabbage palms, under leaves, bushes, and anywhere there were insects. More than once I heard the distressed cries of frogs caught by snakes on the water's edge. Once I sat and watched in fascination while a big water snake slowly swallowed a large frog. (I didn't have anything else to do that day.) Rabbits were ubiquitous. Where you found them, there were snakes, shy bobcats and foxes. Have you ever heard a fox bark?

I never saw a Florida panther on the ranch, but that is not to say that one of these loners didn't see me. Marjorie Kinnan Rawlings described them this way: "Of 'all them wild things out in the woods,' the panther remains the only one in Florida still gilded with the bright legend of fear. I have heard the sound twice...It is the shriek of a vampire woman, an insane shrill tremolo, half laughter and half moan." We had a panther-scratched tree on the south end, but the marks were old. Paw said they were freshened every year. They were high on the trunk, some 7-8 feet high. Crackers tell of times when they were common. They'd catch about anything they could, deer, calves, hogs, rabbits. They would even track humans, especially little ones. Cleo O'Berry, a long deceased Cracker of Highlands County, used to tell about the panther that stalked him as a boy all the way home. It followed him into the sand floor cabin, but something spooked it, causing it to turn and dash out of the house. I don't think Cleo would have been tender anyway. Florida panthers were deadly top-of-the heap predators that could walk up on you before you knew they were anywhere near.

Black bear were common in all of Florida at one time, too. Their numbers thinned out as the pioneers settled in. They are solitary creatures and didn't take kindly to dogs. Occasionally one crossed the ranch. One man told me that two cowboys caught one eating a calf many years ago. They roped him between two horses and killed him with an axe. Tough people and tough times, I guess.

Paw told of a time when he was a young man in Clearwater. He'd heard of a North Carolina dog breeder named Plott who had selectively bred dogs for bear hunting. The Plott Hounds were developed to trail up a bear, circle it, nipping it in the backside to delay it until the hunters could catch up in the chase. He said that he saw a couple of these dogs and asked the owner all about them. He was sure with the kind of nose they reportedly had that they would trail a deer. So he just bought the two dogs from the visitor, loading them into the trunk of his hunting vehicle. Well, it just happened that the circus was in Clearwater at the time. As he drove through town, devilment hit him and his fellow hunter when they saw the chained sideshow bear. He said, "I thought I'd just give them a look to see how they acted when they smelled bear. Well I just barely opened the trunk so they could peek out at the bear. Then all (*expletive deleted*) broke loose...they busted out, opened up and took to the old bear. The poor old toothless thing ran to the end of his chain, wailing "ouuu-ouuuu", as the dogs snapped at him and nipped him in the butt. I guess the circus elephant was a buddy of the bear because he came after the dogs...we jumped into the car and left. The elephant ran the dogs off, saving the toothless bear. They trailed us up, jumped into the trunk and laid down. We got outta there in a hurry. People wuz comin' from everywher'…boy, them dogs would cold run a bear…poor ol' thing." There are still places in Florida where a number of bears roam. They will steal your garbage.

Remembering the creatures I watched during those times alone in the woods brings a flood of warmth to my soul. I was safer there, alone and deep in the woods, than I would have been going up to an ATM in Miami. Like the men of the last four generations before me, I carried a gun, but rarely needed it. Things had a natural rhythm, predictable seasons. The birds flew at certain times. The fish fed at certain times. Their attitudes, languages, manners of living, and reactions to threat were all in a natural order. Trails and paths were used by many different species. There was great diversity, yet unity. The calls of creatures were somehow comforting. There was a quiet assurance in the order of nature. Weather patterns changed, seasons fluctuated, drought and deluge came and went. The creatures had their niches, their timetables, their schedules, known instinctively by them and quietly learned by a young observer.

Cruel things happened, innocents died to perpetuate others, infants were mauled and the old were abandoned. Death came to some, life to others. The deaths of most were not usually due to blood lust, although some species seemed to enjoy the kill for itself, especially the felines and canines. By and large, many things just wanted to be left alone, to go about their business.

But somehow, in the midst of the serious predator-prey games of life, new life springs up, counter current to the law of entropy. There was balance, order and design to the relationships. Some were much more successful in their approaches than others who didn't have their plan for survival completely worked out.

All in all, it was grand to sit alone at dawn or twilight and watch the activity. These times alone in the back woods gave me new insights into nature, on how she works her magic amid the turmoil. Paw's words stayed with me: "We need to work with nature, not against her. Leave a place for the birds, fish and animals. Leave rough, natural places for them to prosper. We're only stewards, Boy. We can't take anything with us. Make it better than the way you found it and you'll have done well." I have sat in many places in Florida and pondered the natural beauty of the animal kingdom. It is impossible to tear up the land and expect all to be well with its natural inhabitants. His words still echo in my heart. I never taste coffee grounds in my cup that I don't remember these times alone in the woods.

Introduction to Gator Hunting

"An alligator is a snake that a committee built."
-HSJ

MY introduction to "gator huntin'", was a unique experience for me. Though the exercise is as common to Crackers as a Saturday night dance, it is not common to city folk or fellas from Kentucky. It started when I once saw Sonny wade off into a deep place with a hook on a pole, trying to hook a "likely dead" alligator. They would lie on the banks or submerged by the edge of the water and catch calves and dogs. This particular one was living in the pond near the house and had killed Biba and Charles' German shepherd. Sonny shot the nuisance on the bank with a high powered rifle. It plunged into the water like a torpedo. I got up on the bank a ways to watch; you weren't going to get me down by the water's edge. I had seen it close enough already. Hubert's brother Curtis and one or two more men were with us. I forgot who they were. After a lapse of about fifteen minutes, they decided that Sonny should go into the water to retrieve the "dead" gator. He was sure he had done it in. I remember his easing into the water, barefooted and shirtless and feeling around with the hook. I was standing at a respectful distance. In retrospect, I don't know what we would have done if the gator had decided to catch him.

Years later, Sonny was examining a legally harvested gator that had been shot. They drug him into the airboat and were calming down from the experience. The gator was completely motionless and appeared dead. Sonny marveled at the teeth of this creature. They intermeshed to form a tight network of holding tools. He casually stuck a finger down to test the texture and intricacy of the area between some teeth. Well, as he discovered, the gator's neural system is reptilian. It works even when body function is disengaged. The gator clamped down his jaws automatically, trapping Sonny's finger in the edge of it. He said they had a devil of a time getting his finger out of the gator's mouth. It took a couple of men and an axe to do the trick. His finger was purple and flat when finally removed. He warned unnecessarily, "Don't put your finger anywhere near a gator's mouth, even when he looks like he's dead..."

Sonny had a thing about fingers. He nearly lost a couple in a power saw accident once. All I remember, as I rushed him to the Emergency Room in the Chevy station wagon, was his saying, "Slow down, the tires on this car aren't very good." He held his hand up, in bandages that were soaked in blood as we raced to the hospital. Doctor Steve came out to the waiting room and pronounced that he had put him back together and that Sonny would never play the violin again; 'Course, Sonny had never played the violin before, so we thought that was okay. The patient did complain that his trigger finger became stiff. All in all, that was a minor thing compared to the glider wreck he had years later. It took several hours of orthopedic surgery to piece his ankles back together. His only complaint then was that he couldn't wear cowboy boots anymore. He truly was tougher than a bus station steak. (I'll try to keep my mouth shut about the bad knee from my slide down the mountain in Montana, since he doesn't complain about any of the steps he takes on those reconstructed ankles.)

It was Sonny who taught me how to catch gators. Since that introduction I have seen other ways. At the time it was legal, but things were different twenty-five years later. People were concerned about their extinction. It became a highly regulated activity. Many an old Cracker made a living out of hunting gators. The skins were valuable and the meat was tasty. Illegal gator hunters lost their boats, their gear, and paid heavy fines or went to jail. The Crackers dryly joked about "Cracker Season," meaning illegal hunting at night or out of the regular season. One might ask, "When does deer season open?" Another might reply, "Oh, about dark tonight..."

The technique we used for calf-killing gators was rather simple. A large gator had taken up residence in a deep water hole on the north side of the ranch and we feared he could too easily get to the baby calves from this perfect ambush point. Sonny made a 6-inch peg out of a piece of hard oak. He tapered both ends, rounding them to blunt points. The peg was probably about one and one-half inches in diameter. In the middle of it he bored a hole into which he inserted the end of small, strong braided-steel cable about 6 feet long. At the peg end he locked the end back on the cable with a solid U-bolt. The loose end he attached to a strong fifteen foot-long nylon rope. We got a dead armadillo, opened his abdominal cavity and placed the peg longitudinally in it. The steel cable came through the skin. We cut a sapling pole, tied the cable to the pole with a light twine, and set it into the hole we'd dug on the edge of the water hole, dangling the armadillo about 6 inches over the water. In effect, it looked like a heavy-duty fishing pole.

The armadillo ripened over the next day. We "ran the trap" to see if Mr. Gator had taken the bait and a day or so later, we found the armadillo gone, the cable pulled off the pole running into the water. The earth had been torn up where the cable went over the edge, clear evidence that a struggle had taken place. The idea was that the gator would grab the bait, chomp on it awhile to soften it up and swallow armadillo, peg and all. As the armadillo digested, the peg was exposed. When the gator tried to get away, the peg turned crossways to his stomach, acting much like a wedge. Sonny gingerly pulled on the rope, feeling the line. The deep water boiled a bit, definite resistance. I got the impression that the gator was digging his feet into the mud. I distinctly remember Sonny's saying, "We best get ready, he ain't gonna take too kindly to being pulled out of his hole." We decided to go for more manpower, a gun and sharp knives. For some reason, I didn't come back for the final activities the next day. I was busy at some other chore, I expect. They caught Mr. Gator and I am certain that the method was a pure Cracker trick. Where Sonny learned it, I don't know. I expect he didn't think I was paying attention at the time. I never forgot it. I swear to this day, if I had to live with nothing in the wild, the Florida woods and waterways are pretty good places. I can see why the Native Americans did so well here.

Sonny could call up gators in the dead of night. We'd ease the airboat into places at an idle, shining our headlights over the dark water. The light reflected on gator eyes and looked like bright rubies on a velvet carpet. Some of these jewels would softly sink into the blackness. Sometimes there'd only be one, other times there were multiple sightings, especially if there was a family of hatchlings. We never bothered them. However, calf or dog killers of size were fair game. The truth is we enjoyed the hunt more than the actual bagging. Most nights we'd come home tired and satisfied with nothing more than that to show for all the work. Sonny could make little grunts that either sounded like a baby calling mama gator or it was so bad an imitation that it made the gator curious. I heard that some Cracker gator hunters carried little terrier-type dogs with them. They called them, "fice dogs". The term was probably a contraction of "feisty". "Fice" as they pronounced it was more correctly, "feist", meaning a lively little housedog. Fice dog apparently is considered a delicacy to alligators. The men clucked to the dog, encouraging him to bark from the bank or boat. The gator just couldn't stand that and would come up to investigate. We had to be quiet to get up close to it. We'd ease up on them just for the fun of surprising them into an explosion when they were touched. Our headlights blinded them so that we could get right on top of them. We'd be cruising along and, suddenly, there would be a volatile boiling under the boat just before we'd get to the gator. By the time he realized we were too close, we'd be on top of him. The larger the gator, the wider the boiling circle.

Some of the old Crackers gator hunted with snare-ropes or cables. As it is told, they slipped up on them in the dark of night, using a spot light, and put a cable snare on the snout before the gator got away. It was a tug of war from then on. Obviously, some judgment and experience was required. It would not be wise to try to catch a twenty-footer in this manner, although the old hunters might try it. Most, however, used good judgment. I've heard that some have caught gators in broad daylight with heavy salt water fishing tackle, using fish or some kind of meat as bait with a tough hook on a steel leader. They'd cast close to a cruising or sunning gator. The reaction is an instantaneous "snap" of powerful jaws. Gators will snap on something before they even know what it is.

But times changed. Gator numbers dwindled. There were fewer legal hunters and the numbers harvested were greatly reduced. The State of Florida regulated the hunting for years and now Florida alligators have made a rapid return to a healthy number, even intruding into populated areas and attacking humans and pets. People think it's fun to feed them marshmallows. In fact, once they get accustomed to humans, one can catch them on salt water fishing tackle, especially after people feed them awhile. Some relocators of nuisance gators use the old fashioned traditional way of catching them at night. The problem only comes when gators lose their fear of man. People, especially little ones, become just another menu item. So don't stick your fingers in a "dead" gator's mouth and don't feed them. Today most all of the nuisance calls are from subdivisions and golf courses.

In the last twenty years, some have even organized properties for commercial alligator production. Hundreds of hatchlings are produced for the leather industry and for the exotic meat market. The tail meat is white, tasty and looks like chicken when fried. I cooked alligator gumbo one time and it was terrific.

I wouldn't take anything for the experience, though I never had the inclination to hunt alligators alone. I guess I was never hungry enough.

The Camp House

"It seems to me that the earth may be borrowed but not bought. It may be used, but not owned. It gives itself in response to love and tending, offers its seasonal flowering and fruiting. But we are tenants and not possessors, lovers and not masters."
-Marjorie Kinnan Rawlings, in *Cross Creek*

SONNY, Hubert, Partner, Purty Jesse, Ugly Jesse and James built a camp house in a thick hammock some 2 or 3 miles from the house. The uncomplicated structure had a trace of Hubert's carpentry skills in it but I don't know who really designed it. I suspect Sonny told Hubert what he and Paw had in mind and turned him loose. It was beautifully simple: rough board and batten with two windows on each wall and one door. The shutters on the screened windows were hinged at the top and a nylon rope ran from the lower outside edge of the shutter through a hole just above the window to the inside. The idea was to pull the rope, thus raising the shutter and either loop the rope over a nail inside the cabin or prop the shutter open with a handy stick outside. Crude, but it worked.

They left the inside walls unfinished and built a kitchen counter, cabinets and sink on the far side away from the door. No running water or electricity, but they put in an old-fashioned hand-cranked pump next to the sink. A raised circular fireplace of concrete blocks, probably six feet across and 18" high, was centered in the room with a huge funnel-shaped chimney made of galvanized sheet metal hung over it. It, too, was made with a pulley system where you could adjust the height by cranking up the ratcheted wench. In the middle of the night, you'd have to either add more logs to keep the chimney drawing or lower the device to draw the ember smoke.

At first, it had only gaslights, but we got fancy later with electricity, a small electric water well and pump, toilet, stove, a ceiling fan and several chairs to supplement the campstools. These cleverly designed stools were made of tooled leather triangles with reinforced corners that hooked over three short wooden legs. The legs were fastened together in the middle with a screw that allowed them to fan out. The collapsible legs fit into the holders and you ended up with a triangular three-legged seat. I thought they were designed to see if visitors had mechanical skill and deductive reasoning powers. You could tell a lot about people from watching them figure out those stools.

The camp house was simple and practical. It served as a place for family gatherings, peaceful isolation and letting the world go by. It was particularly enjoyable for me. I liked to go there alone with the dogs. I left the door open and they could come and go as they pleased, hunting whatever. I'd build a fire, make coffee, sit in a rocker and contemplate something—or not.

There were fold-down bunk beds for overnighting. Falling acorns, twigs and such would rattle the tin roof and wake us up several times at night, while a steady Florida shower would act as a drug. All visitors were thoroughly inspected by the resident spiders. We got used to it. We would hear bulls or other cattle crunching on the dry palm fronds and, starting at twilight, raccoons, armadillos, possums, foxes, squirrels and other night creatures would make their way by. Strangely, deer avoided the place when it was occupied. It was dark there in the thick woods at night, especially on the way to the outhouse.

Outside and to the left of the front door was the grill. It was a WWII landing mat about twenty by five feet. The edges had couplings so that a large number of panels could be locked together. These panels were used by Seabees in the Pacific islands during the war. They could grade a sandy place, slap the panels down, interlock them and land a plane in short order.

Stacked bricks were used to adjust the height of our grill. The woodpile was dutifully stocked by Partner or the Jesses year round. Sometimes church fellowship groups and other small groups would borrow the camp house. They were a little messy, fiddling with the utensils and leaving garbage on occasion. But generally, it was left in an okay condition. I remember sweeping the wood floor out some times. The dirt was a combination of muck and sand. A few oak leaves found their way in, too.

The dogs would come back to check on me from time to time, nuzzling my hand as it draped off the arm of the rocking chair. Another, fearing being left out of any affection, would hog its way in for an ear rubbing. They might stay awhile, though the distant sounds of the night beckoned to them.

Even though the camp house, after completion, was a haven of sorts, especially in bad weather and we thoroughly enjoyed going there, we also liked to cook out in the woods. We'd ride out Saturday afternoon around 2:30 to a good campsite. Paw would pick a place that had a good supply of oak wood nearby, build a big fire and put on a pot of water for coffee. He'd sit down on the Jeep's tailgate or on a fallen tree, drink coffee and wait an hour or two until the coals were just right. He'd cut cabbage palm fans and trim the fan off with his pocketknife. He'd make one end very sharp and the other, thicker end he'd only sharpen a little. We called it a meat stick. One of the ends was stuck in the ground while the other end speared the ribs or steak to hang next to the fire. The meat would sizzle and spit a little as the fat cooked off. A cabbage fan was kept nearby to serve as a place to lay the meat when it had to be rotated or turned. We used wild grapefruit or sour oranges as marinade. We'd find an old wild grapefruit or sour orange tree, some of them 60 years old, and shoot down a couple of the fruit-bearing branches with the .22 for basting the meat.

I'd frequently go with him and so would the kids. They'd play as we drank coffee. I would sometimes slip off into the woods and hunt around or run the dogs. I remember toting back a turkey or two at dark. Most everybody would show up at dark (they knew that was when we'd eat) with sliced pink grapefruit sections, baked beans or potatoes, garlic bread, iced tea and ice, too. Mama might bring her famous pecan pie.

In the pasture by the camp house was a bunch of Purebred Brahma bulls from the pioneer Partin Ranch. The bulls appeared gentle and used to humans, but we didn't get too close to them when they lumbered up where we were cooking to watch us. One night as Paw was bending over a fire, adjusting racks of ribs on a grill and squeezing grapefruit juice on them, one of the bulls came up behind and gently nudged him in the backside. Paw turned around, undaunted, and met the huge thing square in the face, eyeball to eyeball. The bull licked his lips and Paw fed him the half-squeezed grapefruit. He lapped it up with his agile tongue and chewed with relish.

Come to find out, the bulls were halter broke. I'll never forget the excitement of rubbing down one of these massive creatures, feeling the pounds of solid muscle under a thick hide of brittle, coarse hair. He licked me with that massive coarse tongue, likely in appreciation for brushing the flies off his back. His skin twitched as I scratched. His breath was moist and hot and had a slightly sweet, aromatic smell. I learned later that sweet smell was the ketones (fatty acids), released into the blood stream by the liver. It would come out like vodka fumes on his breath. (I know some people think you can't smell vodka, but you can.) He lifted his head ever so slightly for me to scratch the dewlap under his neck. He begged for the fruit like a puppy. He probably was familiar with citrus pulp feed, so the grapefruit tickled his fancy.

Paw said you could stomp your foot near a wild grapefruit tree and a few bulls would amble over to see if it was fruit falling off the trees. They were gentle until you tried to organize them in the cow pens. They then reverted back to a wilder state, much provoked. Can't say I blame them much for that. When something startled him, he'd snort-blow a little. After a time, the bulls that had gathered to observe meandered off, like bored critics at an art gallery. You could hear them grunting at each other and every now and then, a scuffle, usually brief. Sometimes you'd hear long, low bellows way off somewhere. The sounds of the bulls and wildlife carried a long way in the cold nights. They were just locating each other, I guess.

There were trails around the camp house, dozer-cleared many years earlier. One went around into a deep cabbage palm hammock and split. The right fork came out fairly close to the cabin; the left went off to a fence leading to a duck pond. It was a few acres in size, built to hold irrigation water and it also served as a watering hole. Paw told me that the nearby well had spit up fossilized sharks teeth while it was being drilled. There was an old homestead nearby and orange trees, nearly a hundred years old, in a cleared area next to the old chimney. They had to have brought the bricks in from Georgia. The house site was a stone's throw from Taylor's trench, the bivouac site before the Battle of Okeechobee.

During quiet fireside moments at the camp house, Paw told wonderful stories of his experiences, of the times he spent hunting in Sumter County, Florida. It was an isolated bird-hunting paradise at that time. On one of his trips with a friend, they camped next to an unnamed lake. It had rained off and on the whole week prior to their arrival, and water was standing in every low spot. They set up camp and made a pot of pond-water coffee. The mosquitoes began to fog in at twilight-dark, viciously seeking blood meals from any warm-blooded creature they could find. The men fought the onslaught for as long as they could stand it, but ended up in the only refuge, the shallow end of the lake, bodies submerged with only their heads above water. They cut cabbage fans and made little tents to protect their heads. All night they stayed this way. They talked about everything they could think of, dozing off occasionally. I can picture two Crackers in the black waters talking amid thousands of whining mosquitoes, talking about the numbers of little bloodsucking "illegitimates", about the weather, hunting, families, cow hunting and such. He was a master of understatement, "It was a long night…"

Another time he and a friend left Clearwater for a week of bird hunting in the Ocala area. They drove a Model-T Ford; not a pretty thing but it worked well in the woods. It was gangly tall with spindly tires. With a piece of canvas covering the front of the radiator, it could go through fairly deep water. He said sometimes you'd get flooded out. The spark plugs and distributor would get wet and many a time he had to use the starter to crawl out of deep water. (For those of you who don't know this technique, when the engine of a stick-shift vehicle is flooded by water, you can turn the key with the low gear engaged. The motor won't start, but the strength of the starter will turn the wheels and slowly jerk the vehicle forward. I don't know if this worked with all the Model-Ts or if this was a later innovation. It did work with the Jeep, however.)

They arrived in late afternoon, collected firewood, made a small cook-fire, and started coffee water from the pond while they set up camp. Once all set, they had a supper of fried bacon, day old biscuits, lima beans, rice and coffee. A normal camping, but at midnight, things got dicey.

They were awakened by the sounds of vehicles coming through the woods. Paw doused the little fire with the remaining coffee, reached up, slid his shotgun out of the back of the car, and crawled underneath the Model-T. His buddy crawled like a fat rattlesnake into a clump of palmettos nearby.

Two vehicles drove up, shining their lights into the middle of the camp. They shut off their engines and sat silently for several long minutes. It was plain that somebody was up to no good. Paw had had enough of this and he remembered that his shotgun had no shell in the chamber. He wasn't one to act impulsively or irresponsibly, but this might be a bad sort, out for trouble. He quietly pulled back the slide, locking it. After a time, listening to frogs and night sounds, he pushed the locking button in, allowing a shell to slam up into the chamber.

Now, the sound of a shell chambering in a shotgun in the cold night air resonates for a long way. It announces to lawmen and outlaws alike that the doors are now open for business. Men exploded out of the vehicles, diving for cover and squawling out, "Hold up, we're the law! Hold your fire! We're the Sheriff's men!" After some shouted exchanges about who was who and what was what, they cautiously approached. The Sheriff and his posse were looking for a couple of escaped chain-gang prisoners. They had assumed the vehicle and camp belonged to the fugitives. Paw observed, "They ought to have known better. I guess that's what happens when you get store clerks on the posse."

He told us about a so-called "mystery herd" in the area of the limestone outcrops near Ocala. It shook up some folks who talked about it regularly. They described the rumbling of a herd of cattle running through the woods around midnight several nights a month: thundering hooves, starting way off in the distance, progressing toward the hearers and then proceeding off into the night. Inspection of the stampede area in daylight gave no sign of cattle tracks. The ground was undisturbed. But the eyewitness accounts were convincing and some of the locals believed the area to be haunted. Others didn't swallow the reports at all and considered that the moonshine must have been a "bad lot". Theories varied, but "haunted" was to most the simplest explanation. Those who told of it were absolutely sure they heard a herd of cattle running in the night.

One cool night Paw said he heard the "haunted herd". It was as described by others. The hoof beats started off in the distance and came by them, dissipating into the night. He took a torch and went out to look. No sign, but way off in the distance he heard the wail of a train whistle.

The herd would come through when the train went over a bridge many miles away, as if the train had spooked them. It was so far away that you couldn't hear the whistle unless the wind was right and the air was cold. The Ocala area is noted for limestone strata that emerge above ground. He said that the water supply in South Florida depended on what water was taken in at Ocala. Through vast subterranean rivers and channels, water flowed under and through this limestone. In the earlier days in Florida, if one could get a well dug to levels below the limestone strata, free-flowing water gushed up. It may or may not have contained sulfur. If it did, it smelled of hydrogen sulfide, i.e., rotten eggs. You could get used to it, however. In dry years, without the hydrostatic pressure, sinkholes developed from the underground caverns in the limestone.

The railroad bridge had its foundation pilings sunken into the limestone. Obviously, sand would not be stable enough for pilings bearing such weights. Paw theorized that the pilings transmitted the clickity-clack vibrations from the trains going over the bridge through the limestone bedrock, making dull sounds many miles away, like stampeding cattle in the quiet night. The limestone acted as a drumhead of sorts. When he told of this logical explanation, most people accepted it, stating they'd never thought of that, but made sense.

The camp house was a secure place, a harbor of sorts in a sea of activities. It was a place that the family came together on holidays or birthdays or family get-togethers for any reason. The smell of wood fire smoke, of cooking coffee, of ribs or some other meat sizzling on an open fire drew us there. I know it sounds like a dream-world paradise and it was to us all. Many times Paw and I discussed my thoughts and his advice on impending decisions.

What to do with my life, how to decide whether to go to college and what to pursue, and the unpacking of the old baggage from past troubled times were settled there. But I think the thing that meant the most to me was the times we just talked.

During after-supper sessions at the camp house while we rocked and stared into the fire, and drank coffee, Paw related stories of early Okeechobee days, when there was feuding between catfishermen and cattlemen. Men came to town to drink, fist- or knife-fight, socialize and get supplies. He laughingly told of an episode where a man decided to relieve himself in a palmetto patch beside the building. He hooked his heels on the front bumper of a Model T and hung on to the hood ornament. Apparently he figured that he'd have privacy with the nose of the Model T parked in the palmettos. He got all situated with his britches down, leaning out into the bushes. A man was asleep in the vehicle and was awakened by the jostling of the car. He eased up into the driver's seat, carefully put his foot on the floor starter button, and eased the vehicle into gear. With a sudden blast of the engine, in gear, the thing took off through the palmettos. The man on the hood soon discovered he needed both hands to keep his grip. Down the main street they went, "Ah-hooga – Ah-hooga", drawing onlookers, and announcing the show to any and all. Every time the man reached for his britches, the driver would jerk the wheel, causing him to return to his two-handed grip. After a pass or two down the mall, the driver figured he'd had enough, so he aimed at the palmetto patch, kicked the vehicle into neutral, and crashed into the rough grasses, his rider's bare bottom taking the swatting of the palmetto fans as it rolled to a stop. The hood rider was slung off and the driver, thinking he had better take advantage of this window of opportunity, left in a hurry, not even pausing to slam the door. It became common knowledge that one should use the outhouse facilities when one came to town, but even then, it was risky. Sometimes the pranks got a little out of hand.

The first pool hall in Okeechobee was the cause of a lot of interest among the cowboys. They'd pile in to watch or play. Some of them didn't know how to play pool but it was a good meeting place. One Saturday night when the house was full, a man, who by all accounts had been drinkin', climbed up on one of the tables brandishing a pool cue. He started swinging it overhead, slapping his chest, and yelling, "I'm a bad man from Tampa! I can whip anybody in this pool hall." When there was no response, things escalated into, "I'm a bad man from Tampa! I can whip anybody in Okeechobee!" Then, "I'm a bad man from Tampa! I can whip anybody in Okeechobee County!" It still went unchallenged. Swoosh, swoosh...the pool cue sounded overhead as he started hitting his chest harder, saying, "I'm a bad man from Tampa! I can whip anybody in South Florida!"

No challenge emerged from the interested on-lookers. This was real entertainment in the pool hall. As the tirade continued, a little man walked close to the table, the pool cue swooshing over his head. The Bad Man from Tampa kept up the ranting, challenging the entire crowd. The little fella took out three or four pool sticks until he had found one that looked straight. He rolled each one on a table to be sure he'd selected a good straight one, all the while never making any eye contact with Bad Man. He ducked slightly as he walked under the swooshing cue, and upon clearing Bad Man's peripheral vision swung the butt end of the pool cue up, connecting with the back of Bad Man's head. He fell like a sack of cold potatoes. The little man got on the table, patted himself on the chest, grinned and quietly said, "I'm a bad man from Ft. Lauderdale. I can whip anybody in Tampa." There was laughter and slaps on the back as they drug Bad Man out into the night and went back to shooting pool. It was just another Saturday night in Okeechobee.

Apparently, from the tales told about him, Paw's daddy was an intelligent man but not necessarily "woods wise." He had a terrible sense of direction, often getting lost in the woods, even very near camp. He was known to shoot his shotgun in the air a little ways from camp, disoriented and totally lost, to signal his location and need for help. Before a hunt, they usually stopped by the local butcher's shop. After loading up the Model T with all their hunting supplies, his daddy would buy a whole roll of twine, way more than enough to use only for hunting.

In the late afternoon after setting up camp, when everyone was ready to hunt, Granddaddy Williamson would walk a little ways from camp and tie the end of the string to a pine sapling. He'd then unwind it as he went out to find a spot near a turkey roost or deer trail. The plan was to re-wind the string on the way in, ending up at the pine sapling near camp. There, he could see the campfire or hear the men talking and find his way back in.

Well, late one afternoon, Paw was walking in to camp when he came upon the string. He figured this was about half way between the campsite and his daddy. He broke the string there, tied it to a nearby pine sapling and wound it up as he went on into camp. It got darker and darker, to the point that Paw was getting worried. He never said a word to anybody, but began to feel guilty. He heard a shotgun fire off a ways and ambled over, calling every so often so he wouldn't get mistaken for a deer. Well, there sat Daddy on a tree stump where Paw had tied off the string.

"What's the matter, Daddy?"

"Aw, Frank, the sons of (*expletive deleted*) moved camp on me…"

Paw said he never told him that he was the one who fiddled with his string.

There was another time that his daddy had bought the very latest in sleeping cots. He'd mail-ordered it from some outfit up North. It was a cot that could be site-assembled, much like ones seen today in barracks and hunting camps. It had the advantages of compact storage when disassembled, of keeping one off the wet earth after dewfall and was fairly comfortable.

Paw said, "He set the dang thing up and put it right in the middle of the door of the tent. He sure was proud of it." The big tent held four or five men. "We had to step over it or go around the end of it every time we went in or out of the tent." During that day someone killed a huge rattlesnake; Paw cut off the rattles and put them in his pocket.

During the after-supper discussion period that occurs in every hunting camp, Paw slipped away and cut a small palmetto fan. He trimmed off the leaves, fashioning a little bow with the stalk and some string. In the middle of the string, he tied the rattles. He placed the bow near the back corner of the tent, just outside of where his bedroll was located within the tent.

Later in the evening, when all were settled into their bedrolls, with Daddy in his fine cot, smack in the center of the door of the tent, Paw queried, "Marcus, did you move?"

"Naw, Frank. Whut 'er you talkin' about?"

"I thought I felt you move at the foot of my bedroll…"

There was a long silence. Men breathed a little deeper as sleep began to shut down the mind for the day. But the seed had been planted.

"Marcus, I wish you'd quit moving around…"

"Whut? I ain't movin', Frank."

Whisper quiet, Paw slid his hand out under the edge of the tent and grabbed the rattler bow, slipping it in very slowly, so as to not disturb the rattles.

"Dang it! Marcus; quit moving your leg…" (He kicked a little at the foot of his bedroll as if he was trying to get it straightened.)

"I ain't movin' nuthin', Frank…"

Again a long silence as the men watched the flickers of campfire light on the tent ceiling. The stage was set…Paw chose that moment to twang the bowstring. It was a near-perfect rendition of a startled rattler.

Well, there was an explosion of yelling, cursing and thrashing as men scampered out of their bedding. In the scuffle, Daddy's poor cot took a pummeling from rushing bodies and tipped butt over teakettle into the campfire, throwing Daddy, cot and bedroll into the flames. He rolled clear, but by the time the men had collected themselves and pulled it from the fire, the new cot was nearly burned up.

Paw immediately hid the bow and rattlers; he was too ashamed to admit it was another prank backfire. He played along as the men insisted on removing everything from the tent, shaking out bedrolls, looking for the culprit rattler.

"It took mite near an hour before things settled down. They all slept fitfully the rest of the night. Daddy sure was upset about his new cot. I never told him about that either."

Listening to the stories of Paw's life was healing. Mama healed there, too, finding love, acceptance, security and encouragement. Paw told us many things important to him, giving insight into his character. I think he, too, healed in the telling and it helped us all. We three particularly bene-fited from the quiet times, the therapy, there in that isolated hammock, in that crudely built camp house. It was as if we were in another world. You somehow were able to see things in perspective at the camp house. I go there in my mind on occasion, when anxious or just thinking on the past. It's the place where I escape from the troubled world to remember comfort-ing memories. But I know that it can never be the same, for my stepfather is not there anymore. He made the difference. He was the reason that it was a special place for us all.

Well, Boy, You Thought Any More about What You're Goin' to Study in College?

"One of my first roommates in college moved in with us the second semester. At first everything was okay. But then we started noticing things were missing. The first thing was the trash in the trash can. Then the piles of ashes and cigarette butts in the ash trays. Then the dirty clothes and wet towels on the floors disappeared. I never said anything to him, but we never invited him to stay the next semester."
-Adapted From Jack Handley, in *Fuzzy Memories*

SEVERAL months passed. Now, somewhat seasoned as a ranch hand, still green, still having a lot to learn, I had to cut bait or go to th' house, as they say. The University of Florida considered my request for admission seriously. I had to take the next step in going to college. Since I had no in-state schooling records, I had to appear in Gainesville in the fall of 1960 to take college entrance exams. Reeda and Paw went with me. I did okay on the exams, I guess. I passed and was accepted at the University of Florida for the January term of 1961.

Though I wasn't sure what I would eventually pursue in a curriculum it didn't matter the first year. I was informed by the University that courses were fixed in an introductory set of core classes that all freshmen had to take. I wasn't thinking of anything beyond the first semester. On Jeep rides during the summer before I left, we'd discussed how to choose a career. His advice was very practical: "Decide whether you want to work indoors or outdoors; the rest will fall into place." It was simple but I was still unsettled. I pondered this for weeks and months. He helped me stabilize riding in the Jeep, in places of Cracker history, and in the woods and swamps. He had a way of stating things logically. His advice sounded reasonable to me.

One event may have been the deciding factor in my ultimate choice. That summer, as we were working in the pens, Red, Sonny's prize race-winning mare, was saddled and tied near the main gate. She was minding her own business, watchful but resting. Sudden as a summer downpour, there was a bullfight. A Brahman bull decided he would have none of this pen business and determined he would find or make a way out no matter who or what was in his way. He cleared right-of-ways through the little wads of terrified cattle. Men, dogs and chickens scattered, climbing fences or whatever offered escape. The enraged bull caught Red trapped in among a tightly packed group of cows. He vented his rage, hooking her in the right thigh, leaving a gaping hole on the back of it. She kicked wildly, squealing and bouncing away from him. His horns, at their base, had to have been 4–5 inches in diameter, very effective weapons. With his powerful neck behind the gore, he had left a nasty hole with skin hanging from it.

Sonny told me to take her to the local veterinarian, Dr. Frank Platt. I loaded her in the cattle trailer and pulled out for town. The doctor came out of his little office to the shell and marl driveway where I had unloaded Red; she was standing quietly on three legs. He approached her, speaking softly to her so she would know he was there. He put a hand on her rump, easing around, simultaneously sizing her and the wound up. Her gum color was good, which meant she was not in severe shock. She had stopped the severe trembling from the adrenaline surge. But she felt a little clammy to me, a cold sweaty feel to her skin.

Red rolled her eyes at him as he explored the depth of the wound, but allowed it. This was just another day at the office for her. He went back inside and returned with a tetanus antitoxin injection, a penicillin injection and a liquid called "thiouramide," I think. It was a liquid sulfa drug containing urea, serving to clean out the debris and necrotic material. It apparently repelled flies as well. Red didn't seem to mind the wound's being flushed, although she did side-step him some. He gave me instructions for her care. I watched as he patted her neck while holding a needle so he could rotate his hand on the last firm pat and drive it to the hub in her neck muscle. She didn't even flinch. I was impressed.

This was my first time to see a large animal veterinarian in action. I liked him. He talked to me a while, as if in no big hurry. He was calm and easy going, laughing a lot. Here was a potential career, I thought. I really didn't totally fit as a Cracker at the time, not being born to the Florida cowboy culture as were most. I didn't fit as a complete country boy either, since I had lived in downtown Miami for a while, though I hated it. I felt as if I were an in-betweener type, one able to adapt in various environments, but I never forgot Dr. Platt's manner and skill. The thought germinated in my impressionable mind, "This profession might have a place for me."

I didn't realize at the time how much this incident influenced me. I. could see myself doing that kind of work.

On the day I told Reeda and Paw what I had decided to pursue, we were on an appraisal trip and had stopped for lunch at a little diner a just outside of Belle Glade. He'd taken Reeda, me or both of us on many such trips. Large loans were needed by some ranches to develop their property or make improvements. He'd review their business plans, look over the ranch or grove, judge whether they would be able to repay and make recommendations to the office in Hartford. He must have been good at it because they never had a default on any of his approved loans. I really don't remember when he started doing this line of work for Connecticut Mutual Insurance Company, I suspect sometime in the fifties.

Walking in the little cafe felt like we'd been thrown back to the forties. The windows were crank-open affairs. The counter had seats like those of the old soda fountain day, backless stools, chrome trim and shiny red seats. You know the kind, ones that tore like fabric but had a slick surface and mischievous boys liked to punch holes in them with pocket knives. The tables were old but functional, as evidenced by those who were seated at them, enjoying good diner food. The place was bustling with cowboys, locals, shopkeepers and truck drivers. It reminded me of a gold-rush saloon. There was the smell of a grill turning out hamburgers and onions. The place was full of activity. We found our own table. The blackboard said, "Today's Specials." It had a selection of mostly country cooking, such as meats, beans, potatoes, burgers, cobbler, and pie. The tea was sweet.

We ordered from the stereotypical waitress, neat, clean, with a hair net and the little cap like a nurse's. "Whut c'hall want?" she said. She had the soft twang of a pure Cracker girl. Nevertheless, we effectively communicated our choices.

As we waited for our lunches, just looking around, Paw said, "Well, boy, have you thought any more about what you're going to do in college?" After a pause I answered, "Well I've been thinkin'. Why couldn't I do both inside and outside work? I think I'd like to be a veterinarian. It sounds like a tough choice, but I sure think I could do it. How does that sound?"

He studied me a little, saying, "Well, why not get a job with one and see if you really like it. The worst thing that could happen is that you could say you did or didn't want to go that way, and that, my friend, is valuable information." So it was set. I would try a job while starting college. Then, assuming I liked it, make a stab at getting into veterinary school.

The day I was to leave approached way too fast. I was torn between leaving this harbor of joy, really the only home I'd ever experienced and the best imaginable, and stepping into the ocean of the unknown. We toured the campus and I wasn't so sure I wanted any part of it. After the freedom of the woods, it was too fast, too busy, too many people…but I innately knew that it would be for the best. The fact is I really wanted to stay in the safe haven of the ranch.

Under the big oak in the front yard, I'd had a talk about not going to college. We stood there smelling the evening air and quietly talking. I mentioned to him I would be content to skip college and stay on the ranch and work. He did not dismiss this statement out of hand. He idly waved a mosquito off, looked out into the marsh several seconds and rolled the panatela. The smoke slowly curled into nothingness. After a bit, he turned slightly and looked intensely into my eyes.

He said, "Well, Buddy. There are too many variables. There's too much family in this operation now; things have a way of changing. What if something happens to me and Sonny? What if you get seriously hurt and can't work anymore? If things didn't work out here, what would you do? I'll tell you, when you go to get a job somewhere, they more often than not take college graduates over those that don't have a degree. Two men apply for a job, one with a degree in anything and one without. The degree usually gets the job. If you leave, what would you do then? You need to develop something that no one can take away from you. A college degree is yours forever. I believe it is the best thing I could do for you. We'll sell oranges to see that you can go. If we run out of oranges, we'll sell every damn cow on the place for the money to send you."

The mosquitoes were beginning to emerge for the evening hunt. I didn't say much. My heart was breaking a little. It wasn't rejection. I knew he was right—he always was—and I knew he had my best interests at heart. He spit a tiny speck of cigar leaf out on a finger and flipped it. I shifted my weight to the other leg. My boots were still wet from the days' activities. The frogs were waking up for the night shift. A hawk called out in the marsh. The mosquitoes whined like miniature cheap motorcycles.

After a long interval, amid the sounds of the night, he concluded, "Anyway, it's not up to me. You'll have to talk it out with Sonny. He will take over everything someday." I knew there was no reason to talk with Sonny. Paw was right...

Not long after that I packed my necessities for the University of Florida. One of the last things I did was stop by Sonny and Betty's house and tell them good bye. I almost cried when I hugged them. Sonny said, "You take care, Howard. Don't have any fun and study hard." I loaded up and went down the drive slowly, looking at the pastures.

As I drove north on Highway 27 I drove through a small, sleepy town named Sebring. The waters of Lake Jackson nearly lapped the edge of the highway. In my wildest imagination I would have never guessed that I would one day live and work there among some of the finest Crackers a fella could ever hope to know. But that's another book...

Somehow Reeda's man had implanted some self esteem. The odds had been beaten. I was almost whole. Yes, I was more than a little heart-sick when I left; I came there as a broken boy. I left as a mostly healed young man with some confidence and potential. Though I would make many mistakes in the future, I would come out of them for the better. Boy, howdy! I'd come a long way...and I had a long way to go. The hills of Western Kentucky, the farmlands of Indiana and the streets of Miami no longer had a hold on me. I was home at last...

Near the End

"We know not what we shall be, but we may be sure we shall be more, not less, than we were on earth. Our natural experiences (sensory, emotional, imaginative) are only like the drawing, like penciled lines on flat paper. If they vanish in the risen life, they will vanish only as pencil lines vanish from the real landscape, not as a candle flame that has been put out but as a candle flame which becomes invisible because someone has pulled up the blind, thrown open the shutters, and let in the blaze of the risen sun."
-C.S. Lewis

TWENTY YEARS passed in a flurry. My college experience included the University of Florida's School of Animal Sciences, Auburn University's School of Veterinary Medicine, five years of private practice in Highlands County, in the heart of Cracker country, and a residency in Dairy Medicine and Surgery at Auburn with a Ph.D. in Animal Science, Ruminant Nutrition. Paw was right: college opened up great opportunities.

Sonny appreciated my humor about the Ph.D. Things like, "There's a 95% chance that what I am telling you is 90% true." Paw told my mother, "It was just like that boy to jump in the deep end. I just had a feelin' he'd push ever way he could. Nobody can accuse him of not settin' his sights high." But he was proud of me. Though he wasn't one to flatter or verbalize praise much, he was pleased with my achievement, saying that a Ph.D. meant, "Piled Higher and Deeper." He had this sweet smile on his rough sunburned face when he said it, like he knew I enjoyed it and I did laugh every time. Danged if he wasn't right about that. I had moved up from, "Dog Vaccinatin' Man", to "Piled Higher and Deeper."

During the last seven years of his life while my wife, Hunter, our daughters, Madeleine and Catherine, and I were at Auburn, we visited the ranch as often as possible. Sonny and Paw decided to locate some property in Alabama, to expand and diversify the ranch. Auburn was about 2 hours away, so every time they came up, we'd get together. Reeda and Paw attended my Animal Science graduation ceremony in August of 1980, two years before he passed away. He summed up five years of hard academic work by simply saying, "Son, you did real good." That meant as much as the sheep-skin diploma—more, in fact.

But somewhere, sometime in his late seventies, an abnormal cell divided in my stepfather's body. No, it was not related to cigar smoking. Ordinarily we all have a few abnormal cells here and there. We're bombarded by all sorts of unfriendly cosmic rays, rampaging free radicals and toxins and chemical insults. The astounding phenomenon is that we all don't die of cancer. A healthy immune system and other biochemical mechanisms can take care of most of these freakish occurrences. As we age or if we're hampered by a dysfunctional immunity due to poor nutrition, questionable health habits and sedentary living, these freak cells may become like a runaway train.

When normal cells are overwhelmed by a particularly aggressive division of one in a critical area of the body, a real psychotic malevolence develops, one that kills all it touches. Sometimes we can apply the brakes if caught early enough. In my stepfather's case, since he never complained much, the runaway cells were left to gather downhill momentum at an ever increasing speed.

I don't recall when Hunter and I were first told of his diagnosis. There wasn't much said other than he was being treated by radical surgery and chemotherapy. Reeda and Sonny were handling all the details. I really didn't have much insight into the seriousness of the cancer until it was clear that he was in real trouble. I don't think the family realized it either. However, things got out of control very rapidly. He endured the indignity of the surgery, the hospitalization and the intravenous as-bad-as-the-disease chemotherapy. His spirit was not broken but he was suffering. When all was done that could be done, he came home to the ranch. Hours of pain and agony would follow, somewhat lessened by modern medications, but still the pain had a life of its own as the cancer moved from system to system.

When the disease was clearly well advanced, Sonny told me that Paw wouldn't make it much longer. Upon receiving this bad news, I was seized with a strong compulsion to see him. He'd been brought home to finish his time on earth. Leaving my staff duties at Auburn, I spent a week with him just before he died. It was one of the most wonderful times we'd ever had together, and we'd had some doozies. He was not able to do much. He'd have bouts of such severe pain that he was incapacitated. Mama would give him a potent narcotic tablet. He'd sleep sitting up in his recliner for a time. Finally, he'd wake up, look around and settle his twinkling eyes on me. He'd start out with a smile, like he was glad I was there, "How you doin', buddy?" and he'd begin talking. He'd go on about Florida, the ranch, the kids, history and people he'd known. I would give anything to have a recording of it all now. He wouldn't have loosened up if he'd known I was recording it, I expect. He was rather private sometimes. But much of what I relate in this story comes from these few days toward the end, with the two of us just talking. Jeep rides were out of the question then, though I suspect he'd just as soon leave the earth out on the ranch as he had in a bed.

One of the difficulties of metastatic cancer is the infiltration and loss of function of other organ systems. He had a problem with bowel control. He'd not make it to the bathroom in time. This happened on one occasion while I was there. So Mama took him into the bathroom, put him in the shower and gave him a good scrubbing. She dried him; put his pajamas on him, warm from the dryer, and finished up with a terry-cloth robe. She combed his hair back like he liked it and put his feet in his favorite slippers.

He padded back into the living room, smelling like a lily, stopped just past the doorway, looked over at me and panted, "Boy, it's hard when you're pizzle-sprung." Now the term "pizzle" is an old English and Australian term for damage to the reproductive organ of the bull or ram. The "pizzle-sprung" bull or ram can't breed.

We laughed out loud. Even in the throes of terminal cancer, he retained his humor. Mama cared for him, doing little things to make him comfortable. Once, he paused, looked at me and said, "Boy, your mama's a good woman. Sometimes a fella has to go through two or three of them to get a good 'un." She laughed when he said it. The doctors told him, "Sir, you can't smoke. It's bad for you." He said, "Well after all I'm eighty years old. What's it gonna do now?" In the hospital he'd told one nurse who was trying to pass a urinary catheter, "You'd better get some tweezers if you want to do that right."

The call came to our bedside phone in Auburn the night of October 9, 1982. Sonny simply said, "Paw's gone, Howard." He went on quietly giving the details for the funeral. He said, "Reeda is holding up pretty well, as good as can be expected, I guess." I remember hanging up the phone, telling Hunter, "Well, his suffering is over now; he's gone." We cried a little, there in the dark in East Alabama. I knelt by the bed and prayed, thanking God for relieving his pain, for the man, for the sheer grace of knowing him for a little while, for the family and for the ranch.

Feelings of devastating emptiness, void, and loss took me for a time. But somewhere intermixed with these feelings were soft melodies of gratitude and hope. For a time I felt as if I would never recover from his loss. Once again, I healed, knowing he'd say, "Git on with yer life, Boy."

He'd not complained of anything, as far as I know. I had written my stepfather a personal letter after hearing about the diagnosis. I poured out my heart to him, telling him how much I appreciated his loving my once-bruised mother and for his patience with her and me. I expressed things that would have embarrassed both of us if delivered in person. I told him that I was about the luckiest man I knew, that I had a real father – one who had adopted me like my heavenly Father. The letter was written just before I went to sit with him the week in September of 1982. He never mentioned it. I thought it had embarrassed him. At the funeral, the pastor, Rev. Dick Whipple, read my letter. Being somewhat overwhelmed at the time, I remember it expressed my gratitude for his compassion, unconditional love and leadership. I was astounded that Paw valued it so much.

After the funeral there were many decisions to make, meetings to attend, and the baton was handed to Sonny and Wes. It was up to them to carry on in transition, a plan Paw had worked on for over twenty years. Reeda continued to live on the ranch for a time. She said at times she thought she could hear him shuffling through the empty house. The house was the same, the family was the same, the ranch was the same, but a great void existed, a palpable emptiness.

We all wanted to bury Paw on the ranch but State regulations set so many restrictions that Sonny elected to have him buried just outside the west gate at the county cemetery on Taylor Creek. It would have been fitting for him as a pioneer to be buried on the ranch he so loved. If I'd had my druthers we could have taken his body on a horse-drawn wagon, ol' Dixie with empty saddle tied behind it, and buried him by the massive oak that he rescued from the dozer in the early forties. But he can at least be close to the ranch. To be honest, my visits have declined over the years. It is not the same. Who was it that said, "You can't go home again"? Thomas Wolfe?

To me, the ranch is still wonderful, but incomplete without him. The one who'd reclaimed my life is not there. I've asked myself at times, "Could I make it? Had he been able to accomplish good in me?" Yes! "Had he indeed altered my course in life in his taking a boy and growing a man?" Most certainly I thought he had. I think he has given a part of his life to me, choosing to love me as a son. I will forever marvel at that grace. Even as painful as it is to remember the loss of him, I still am full of joy at the experience of having known him for those brief twenty-two years, those remarkable and life-changing years. The embers of them are still warm in my healed heart. It was the end of a significant life, a pioneer dynasty, and a most grand time for us all.

My imagination is not good enough to have conceived of a more magnificent story than that of my stepfather talking to me under an oak tree in that old green Jeep. How many have ridden horseback, hat brim down, with a yellow slicker flapping in a violent thunderstorm or hurricane? How many have worked all day in the hot sun in the pens or sat in the Florida woods at twilight, listening to the owl hoot, the frogs awaken singing, while dogs ran looking for a race? How many have laughed hard at the antics and humor of Cracker cowboys? Few have had the extraordinary blessing of working in the Cracker culture, and fewer still will do so in the future. I couldn't resist giving a little taste of it to you.

All these wild and wonderful things and much, much more I have experienced. My life really became worth having because of the grace, mercy, care and nurturing of one man on earth, under that tree, in a green Jeep. He was the one that took me as I was and saw me as I could be. He was my stepfather, my friend and my father—Frank Wesley Williamson, Sr. Yeah, I know he was human. Like us all, he had his flaws.

But as he would say to me, "Boy, it was a hellava ride, wadn't it?"

Epilogue

I am not a cowboy now—don't pretend to be, but I am most at ease in that rough country and feel comfortable in my own skin when I'm surrounded by that rough environment. It's where I go when I'm confused… and all I can see is way off in the distance on the earth around me in the daytime and a long way off in the distance in the night sky above me. It is there and then I know I am not lost.
Robert Fulghum, in *Maybe (Maybe not)*

Forty-five years, nine months and four days after the oak tree talk, I made a trip to the ranch in my new green Jeep. After spending the night in the guest house, I loaded up way before daylight, and rode out like we used to do. At 5:00 a.m., somehow, it felt like I was going to work again. I drove to town for breakfast, eating alone and in reflective silence alongside some cowboys and fishermen. I traveled north to the cemetery, just outside the ranch's south gate. The tombstones read:

Frank Wesley Williamson, Sr.   *Reeda F. Williamson*
October 26, 1902   *June 19, 1920*
October 9, 1982   *June 1, 2000*

After driving slowly by Hubert's grave in the motionless morning air, I looked unsuccessfully for Partner's, then returned to the ranch by the back road. Memories came rushing through me as I drove by the old machine shop where we'd meet before work, where Hubert's bulldog settled the argument with the Ridgeback and he affectionately like to have squeezed me to death. It was the same place where the men cut off my shirttail, for <u>not</u> shooting at a deer. It is filled with rough lumber, sawn out of downed trees from the 2005 hurricanes that did so much damage in Florida. The sweet guava trees are gone.

I eased out at a pace that mimicked the original green Jeep and passed the first bridge and the clay pits whose marl materials were used to make the original roads on the ranch, and where Luther fished for the mythical Grand-daddy Bass. I went by the first grove, the little duck pond and the well that started my well-painting career. I passed the place where I fell off the horse in front of Sonny and where I lost my nearly new rope. I crossed the bridge we had built near the "Oak of Compassion" that Paw saved from the dozer with his handkerchief. I went through the double gates toward the Four Hundred and Walkup's Island Grove. The Four Hundred is where Shug saved my bacon that day. A huge turkey gobbler was out strutting his stuff, all by himself. He saw me, but continued his dance. Shutting off the engine I just watched him prance around, calling to no one in particular. I remembered a time when that gobble would have excited me to no end during hunting season. I went by Walkup's Island and the grove on the right just beyond it and proceeded out into the marsh on the south side of the ranch. I could see the dairies across the fence. I rode past the big pine where Paw said there used to be a panther scratch, and through the marsh which Wes is planning to return to wetlands. Then onto the road which borders the fence. The road was rougher than I remembered; the Jeep bounced just like I was planting seed again.

I eased around the fine cattle and their newborn babies. They weren't afraid at all. I went to the oak field at Opal where the set of giant choppers sat in tandem. They didn't look as if they had been moved since I stood between them waiting on two turkeys to come by, some forty years ago. At Opal, going to the old railroad grade, I turned right, going through the gate. The old maps show a place near Opal called Old Camp Starvation, named by hungry surveyors no doubt. I stopped to drink the sulfur water from the artesian well there. It was slightly warm, steaming some in the cold morning air. It tasted familiar and brought back memories of times. Through the opening in the brush at Opal I meandered onto the higher ground of the piney woods that the English exploited. The Pine Beetle infestation has taken a tremendous toll on the pine there. Few healthy pines remain but the undergrowth has made it a mass of tangled vegetation that couldn't be ridden on horseback now. I rode past the places I'd chopped and cleared with the dozer.

On the bank of the Duck Pond, near the well that had spit up the fossilized shark's teeth, I sat for several wonderfully quiet moments. The yearling bass darted around, but ignored me after their initial frenzy. Remnant trees of the homesteader's orange grove were still there. The sour-orange trees look even rattier; they must be way over a hundred years old. Most have died out.

Toward the camp house, I saw the imprint of hurricanes—hundreds of cabbage palms piled haphazardly like fallen Celtic warriors at the foot of Sterling Castle. I couldn't drive where I used to for the tangles and road-blocks. I detoured to the camp house. It seemed smaller and older and worn, as if it hadn't been used for some time. I got out and worked my way through the woods over trees and palms obstructing the old trails. I got disoriented some, but had the sun and old memories to go by. I walked right up on a lone turkey. He was as startled as I was and left in a hurry. The woodpeckers were going about their pecking business. Squirrels were in their usual hurry. I took a severe cussing from one of them amid the treetops.

Going back out toward the marsh, I went to the tree where Paw and I had our first real talk, where a man took in a boy because he loved his mother. It is right near the canal crossing we used to cut through to the horse barn. While I rested there I spent some time looking out and around, squinting in the bright sun. The oak tree is not as defined as I remember it. The fencing has been replaced and moved a little. There was more underbrush there now. I came out and headed to the house, both satisfied and emotionally jumbled.

Times have changed; the ranch has, too. A second, third and fourth generation carry on under new rules of engagement. I wouldn't take anything for the experience I had there. Though not all was perfect and romantic, it was a life changing time for me. I guess I will be most content if I can just take my grandchildren there someday when they're old enough for a camping trip and a walkabout.

You could never guess what came in the mail today, the very day that I was finishing this Epilogue. David's wife, Maury, sent me a picture of Paw, taken by Biba in the early sixties, standing alongside the green Jeep. Smokey is trying to nuzzle his right hand for an ear rubbing. His hat is creased and neat. A car that looks a little like the white Cadillac is parked in the background. He's got on his sunglasses, a light jacket, a white shirt opened at the top button, the twill britches, and those Wellington boots. His left hand is on his hip, thumb in the belt, showing the wedding ring he later lost in the concrete in the grove. He looks exactly like I remember him the first day I met him, except for the hat. He has a smile on his face and, if I know him like I think I do, he was grumbling under his breath, "Git it over with, Biba."

Can you imagine what this does to my heart? I can just hear him saying,

"How you doin', buddy?"

Paw, Smokey and Jeep

Howard Selby Jones was born in Henderson, Kentucky, and moved to south Florida during his teen years. After two years at the University of Florida, he was accepted at Auburn University School of Veterinary Medicine where he gained his DVM. Following a stint in the Veterinary Corps in the United States Air Force and five years in a large/small animal partnership in south Florida, his teacher's heart brought him back to Auburn where he completed a two-year Dairy Medicine and Surgery Residency while earning his PhD in Ruminant Nutrition in the Department of Animals Sciences. After one year as the Dairy Extension Specialist for the Alabama Cooperative Extension Service, he purchased his former Florida practice.

For the following twenty years, he covered over a fifty mile practice radius surrounding Highlands County in the heart of his beloved Cracker cattle country. Now retired, Dr. Jones lives in the Blue Ridge Mountains of Western North Carolina with Hunter, his wife of forty-two years. They boast of three children and six grandchildren.